The McCauley Family in Philadelphia

Including the

Wallace & Patton Families

from Mullaghinch,

County Londonderry, Ireland

The McCauley Family in Philadelphia

Including the

Wallace & Patton Families

from Mullaghinch,

County Londonderry, Ireland

Kathryn Chambers Torpey
Alexandria, Virginia

Kathryn Chambers Torpey is a professional genealogist and researcher.

Other Books by Kathryn Chambers Torpey:

John Kennedy of County Donegal, Ulster, Ireland, and His Descendants - A Compiled Genealogy (Including Risk, McCoy, and Pendleton), 2006

William Kennedy of Chester County, Pennsylvania, and His Descendants - A Compiled Genealogy (Including Davis, Smith, Wallace, Russell, and McClure), 2014

Colonial and Revolutionary Kennedy Families from Southeastern Pennsylvania, 2015

The Edwards/Scott Family History - Edinburgh to Philadelphia, 2016

The Chambers Family in Philadelphia Descended from George Chambers Born c 1815 in Ireland, 2016

The Reitze Family in Philadelphia Descended from Christopher Reitze Born 1824 in Hesse-Cassel, Germany, 2017

The Devlin Family in Philadelphia Descended from Peter Devlin Born c 1810 in Ireland (the female perspective), 2018

Imprint: Kindle Direct Publishing Platform

ISBN-13: 978-1729635780
ISBN-10: 1729635784

Torpey Books
5035 Domain Place
Alexandria, VA
22311-5066

IN MEMORY OF -

Emma Wright Berger
William Scott Chambers
Willis Skillman McCauley, Jr.
Marion Elaine Muller Wilson

- four of the great-grandchildren of Stephen and Margaret (Wallace) McCauley.

*Without their help, writing this
family history would have been far
more difficult.*

Contents

INTRODUCTION

This family history documents the life of Stephen and Margaret (Wallace) McCauley and their three children, James, Thomas and Margaret.

The narrative begins with a description of the early history of the McCauley family in County Londonderry, Ireland. It then describes their decision to leave home, their journey to America, and their life in Philadelphia after the arrival of the family in 1849. The family history concludes with a profile of each of the three adult children of Stephen and Margaret (Wallace) McCauley.

The purpose of the narration is to document for posterity the sequence of major events in the life of the McCauley family; to bring them back to life, albeit only momentarily; and to depict their fundamental character and outlook on life as Scots-Irish Presbyterian immigrants to America.

The research for this family history was conducted in three general time frames. The first family tree was compiled by my father, William Scott Chambers, in the 1950s. It was based on oral tradition in the McCauley family which stated that Stephen McCauley and Margaret Wallace were married in Londonderry, Ireland, and that Stephen McCauley had died in 1902 and been buried in Mount Moriah Cemetery. My father was also in possession of various cemetery deeds, baptismal certificates, and marriage certificates including Stephen and Margaret (Wallace) McCauley's original certificate of marriage dated July 11, 1848, which was prepared by the Session Clerk of the Presbyterian Church in Aghadowey, County Londonderry, Ireland.

Nothing more was done to document the family history until about 1985 when Willis Skillman McCauley, Jr., enlisted the aid of his maternal cousin, Bernard Erl, an experienced genealogist, to research the McCauley family history. Mr. Erl conducted most of his research work at the National Archives North-East Regional Center in Philadelphia, the Philadelphia City Archives, and the Free Library of Philadelphia. It resulted in Mr. Erl preparing extracts from the 1900 and 1910 population census schedules for the McCauley, Wright, and Patton families. He also obtained a letter from Mount Moriah Cemetery concerning the names and dates of death of family members buried in Thomas McCauley's plot, and he made extracts from the *Philadelphia Public Ledger* and the *Philadelphia Inquirer* of relevant obituaries as well as extracts from the death registers at the Philadelphia City Archives for these same McCauley family members. Copies of all this information was provided to me contemporaneously by Willis Skillman McCauley, Jr.

The balance of the original research contained in this family history was conducted between 1995 and 1998 in Washington, D.C., at the National Archives, the Library of Congress, the National Genealogical Society Library, and the Daughters of the American Revolution Library. Research was also conducted at the Latter-Day Saints Family History Center located in McLean, Virginia, and correspondence was carried out with Mount Moriah Cemetery in Philadelphia, and the Pennsylvania Vital Statistics Office in New Castle, Pennsylvania.

Site visits were made to the Presbyterian Historical Society, the Free Library of Philadelphia, and the Philadelphia City Archives all located in Philadelphia. A visit was also made to Arlington National Cemetery in Arlington, Virginia, to locate the grave of Robert Berger, Stephen and Margaret (Wallace) McCauley's great-grandson who was killed during World War II on Christmas Day, 1944, in Cherbourg, France.

Many thanks for providing their recollections for this family history are due to the following four great-grandchildren of Stephen and Margaret (Wallace) McCauley: Emma (Wright) Berger, William Scott Chambers, Willis Skillman McCauley, Jr., and Marion Elaine (Muller) Wilson. Marion Elaine (Muller) Wilson also provided copies of all the family information pages in the *Wright Family Bible*.

As a result of this research, all of the descendants of Stephen and Margaret (Wallace) McCauley were located and some of the enigmas of the family history were resolved.

Kathryn C. Torpey
December 23, 2018

McCAULEY - WALLACE - PATTON DESCENDANT CHART

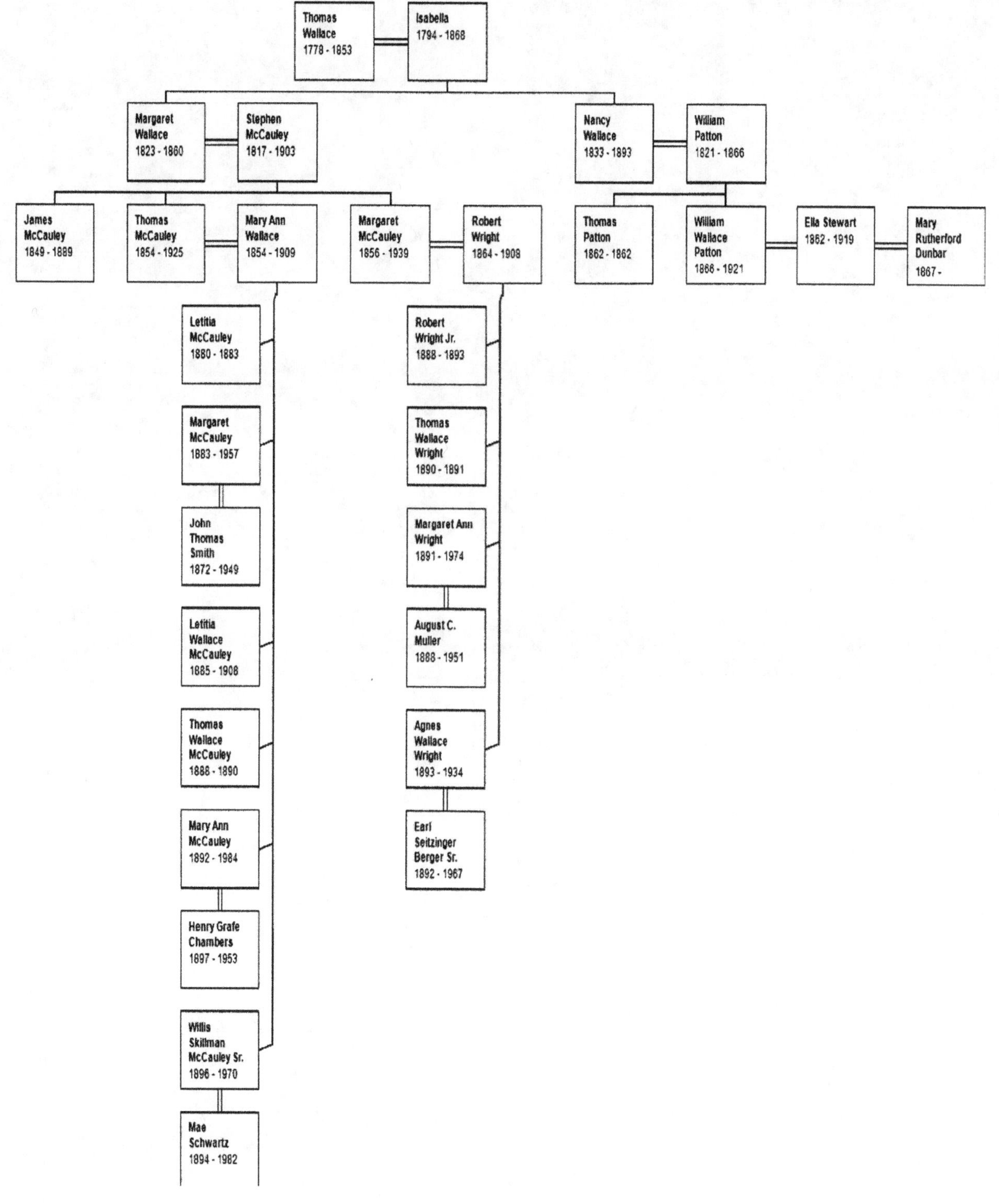

The McCauley Family History

In early September of 1849, a small ship sailed into Lower New York Bay carrying Stephen McCauley, his wife, their infant son, and several other family members. They were coming to America from Ulster (known today as Northern Ireland). The place they left behind, the place they and their ancestors called home for over 200 years, was the townland community of Mullaghinch situated on the Agivey River just south-east of the town of Aghadowey. Their tiny community was located in the civil parish of Aghadowey (which is part of the half-barony of Coleraine) in County Londonderry.

THE PLACE CALLED HOME

Eighteen years earlier, in 1831, it was recorded in a census of church membership that there were 286 people, comprising 54 families, living in Mullaghinch.[1] The census also revealed that 19 residents of Mullaghinch were members of the Established Church, 53 were Roman Catholics and 214 were Presbyterians. Notwithstanding some evidence of limited religious diversity in the townland, the residents were obviously overwhelmingly Presbyterian and of a particular frame of mind - uniformly puritan and conservative - in which their religion was highly important in providing the criteria by which most other aspects of their lives were judged.

Although Stephen McCauley and his wife descended from lowland Scots who had migrated to Ireland during the time of the plantation of Ulster in the 17th Century, they did not think of themselves as Scottish. They considered themselves Irish Protestants and their allegiance was to Ireland. They were industrious, thrifty, and self-reliant.[2] They spoke an English dialect with a distinct rural Ulster accent (as opposed to Gaelic) and they did not mix with the Catholic population.

Earning a Living

Stephen McCauley's occupation is recorded in the ship passenger list as a laborer. However, the occupation of everyone in steerage was recorded as a laborer, women, infants, and children included. Nothing more is known for certain about the exact nature of Stephen McCauley's occupation except that in Aghadowey parish in 1837 laborers generally did one of three things - they farmed the land as tenants or cottiers, they bleached or wove linens known as

---

[1]1831 Church Census of Ireland, County Londonderry, Parish of Aghadowey, Townland of Mullahinch (sic), pages 51-54, FHL Microfilm Roll 0597160.

[2]Kerby A. Miller, *Emigrants and Exiles - Ireland and the Irish Exodus to North America,* (New York: Oxford University Press, 1985), 39.

Coleraines, or they made bricks which were manufactured in this area in considerable quantity.[3]

The townland of Mullaghinch, being located on the Agivey River, was principally a farming community. Barley, oats, potatoes, and flax (for the linen industry) were the chief crops under cultivation.[4] The climate was generally mild ranging from a cool 40 degrees Fahrenheit in January to a warmish 59 degrees Fahrenheit in June.[5] The rainfall was abundant in all seasons giving the landscape in Mullaghinch a rich, green color. Given that the land was fertile and in a high state of cultivation, some of the families were undoubtedly middle-class and at least two were fairly prosperous as they had servants.[6]

If Stephen McCauley was a farmer, he was probably at the bottom of the farming hierarchy. That is, he was either a tenant farmer (known as a smallholder) who leased a small parcel of land from a larger, wealthier tenant farmer who leased the land directly from the Ironmongers Company of London or he farmed lands leased in joint tenancies with other family members who lived in Mullaghinch.[7] Given the likelihood that Stephen McCauley's land would have been of limited acreage (2 to 10 acres), he probably was engaged in little more than subsistence farming. He would have earned the money to pay his high rents by hiring himself out as a laborer to a wealthier farmer during planting and harvest times or he and his wife could have participated in the domestic spinning of yarn that they later sold to the linen weavers in Coleraine.[8] He may not have been able to afford the luxuries of crop rotation or even fertilizing his fields. And, if he didn't own a horse or a plow, he would have depended on the help of his relatives or neighbors to till the fields by hand with primitive spades adapted for use with bare feet. Like everyone else, he and his wife probably lived in a thatched roof cottage with an earthen floor and few rooms and windows. Their furniture would have been primitive. They would have subsisted largely on oatmeal rather than potatoes.[9] Their clothing would have been homespun or they would have purchased used clothing from market town traders in Garvagh or Kilrea.

---

[3]Samuel Lewis, *Topographical Dictionary of Ireland, Volume II,* (London, 1837; reprint, Baltimore, Maryland: Genealogical Publishing Company, 1984), 15.

[4]Miller, 36.

[5]Miller, 9.

[6]1831 Church Census of Ireland, County Londonderry, Parish of Aghadowey, Townland of Mullahinch (sic), pages 51-54, FHL Microfilm Roll 0597160.

[7]Miller, 49-50.

[8]Miller, 36, 372.

[9]Miller, 282.

In the unlikely event that Stephen McCauley was not a tenant farmer, he could have been part of a class of bound laborers known as cottiers - workers who received a cabin and a few acres of land in return for a stipulated number of days' service in the fields or at the looms of the wealthier farmers who employed them.[10] Most cottiers had no leases and rarely handled cash as their employers deducted the rents owed from their wages. Their rents were high, but their land was sufficient for subsistence. On the eve of the famine, cottiers composed the majority of Ireland's rural laborers.[11]

Whatever his occupation, the evidence points to Stephen McCauley being poor, but not so destitute that he could not afford the cost of passage to America for himself, his wife and his son on an American-owned ship at twice the price of passage on a foreign flagship bound for British North America where the provisions of the American Passengers' Act did not apply. And, if he did not pay for the passage himself, help probably came from his relatives in Mullaghinch or from those already in America rather than from an absentee landlord who desperately wanted to clear the land of its destitute tenant farmers by paying for their passage out of Ireland on a coffin ship bound for Quebec.

Deciding to Leave Home

Stephen McCauley's incentive to immigrate to America in 1849 was probably the result of a combination of factors. First and foremost, he was no longer single. He had a wife and infant son to support. This was undoubtedly a powerful motivator in combination with two years of increasingly bad harvests, continuing high rents, downturns in the linen industry, and, most importantly, the ever escalating feeling that he and his family were being treated as second-class citizens by the Anglican establishment in a country his ancestors had helped defend on no less than three occasions in the 17th Century. With the added responsibility of a wife and infant son, Stephen McCauley must have come to the inescapable conclusion that life at home was not likely to get any better any time soon. In fact, living conditions were getting worse every day. There was, therefore, nothing to lose by leaving and everything to gain or so it would have seemed from the letters they were undoubtedly receiving from relatives in America.

JOURNEY TO AMERICA

The ship that brought the McCauley family to America was named the Barque William Chase.[12] It was an American-owned, 256 ton, three-masted sailing vessel built entirely of

---

[10]Miller, 51.

[11]Miller, 52.

[12]Entry for the McAlay Family, Barque William Chase Passenger Manifest, September 7, 1849, p. 2, lines 22-28, Passenger List of Vessels Arriving at New York, NY, 1820-1897, National Archives Microfilm Publication M237, Roll 83.

wood[13]. The two forward masts were square-rigged and the rear or Missenmast was rigged fore-
and-aft. Based on its registered tonnage, its size was only 25,600 cubic feet so it probably was
not more than 115 feet long with a breadth of about 20 feet and a depth of 14 feet.[14] The master
was Captain William Sweetser. The ship was subject to the provisions of the American
Passengers' Act passed by the Congress of the United States during the early years of the potato
famine to protect Irish immigrants from contracting typhus and other deadly diseases due to
overcrowded conditions on the sailing vessels.[15] In theory, this ship was faster, safer, better
equipped, and sailed by a more competent crew than foreign flag-ships sailing to British North
America.

     The passenger manifest of the Barque William Chase indicates that the family embarked
at the Port of Londonderry along with all the other passengers. There were five cabin passengers
all of whom were United States citizens. Everyone else, including the McCauley family, was an
Irish citizen traveling in steerage. Stephen and Margaret (Wallace) McCauley were 32 and 26
years old, respectively. They boarded the ship in the company of three other McCauleys -
Elizabeth (55), Noel (19) and Sally (26) - and a young man named Thomas Wallace (20). They
were probably all related.

     Stephen and Margaret (Wallace) McCauley had been married for about a year when they
set sail for America. In addition to their son, James, and their luggage, they were carrying with
them an extract from the marriage register of the Presbyterian Church at Aghadowey which
stated that their marriage had been solemnized by the Reverend John Brown on July 11, 1848,
according to the form of the Presbyterian Church in Ireland.[16]

---

[13]Entry for the Barque William Chase, September 7, 1849, Target 8, Register of Vessels
Arriving at the Port of New York from Foreign Ports, 1789-1919, National Archives Microfilm
Publication M1066, Roll 6.

[14]The British "Act of Parliament 1854" set a ship's registered tonnage as the internal
capacity of a ship measured in cubic feet divided by 100. This act legalized a practice that was
just about the same in the United States and other seafaring nations. So, the registered tonnage of
a ship is a measurement of volume, not weight. This measurement of volume (or cubic capacity)
defined the earning capability of a merchant ship and was used then (and is still used today) to
assess taxes and port charges.

[15]Edward Laxton, *The Famine Ships - The Irish Exodus to America,* (New York: Henry
Holt and Company, 1996), 30.

[16]Extract of the Marriage Register, Aghadowey Presbyterian Church, County
Londonderry, Ireland, July 11, 1848, original in the possession of Kathryn C. Torpey, 5035
Domain Place, Alexandria, Virginia 22311.

The Barque William Chase probably departed from the Port of Londonderry on August 5, 1849. There is no record that it stopped at Liverpool or any other port before exiting the Irish Sea and sailing west 3,000 miles across the Atlantic Ocean.

The voyage cost about 3 pounds, 6 shillings (U.S. $17.50) per passenger in steerage.[17] Conditions on board were primitive, at best, for the 126 travelers in steerage. The water ration was on the order of 6 pints per person per day to drink, wash and cook. For each week of the voyage, each passenger was entitled to a total of 7 pounds of bread, biscuit, flour, rice, oatmeal or potatoes. Obviously, this was not enough food and water for the crossing, particularly if the ship was delayed on account of bad weather, so passengers needed to bring along some of their own food and water, and maybe even their own cooking utensils, if they planned to survive the voyage. Twice a week, sugar, tea, and molasses were supposed to be distributed to the passengers.[18]

Everyone slept below deck in the hold of the ship on wooden bunks (6 feet long and 2 feet wide) lined with straw.[19] Along with everyone else, the family's belongings, including a trunk that was kept in the family for many years, were stacked in the aisles. There was little to no privacy. Sanitary conditions were fair to poor. Cooking was done on deck. Eating was done below. There was no lighting at night except for a few smoky lanterns. Bad weather may have lengthened the trip. Births, deaths, and illness at sea were not unusual. Given these frightful conditions, the family undoubtedly lived for the duration of the voyage in constant fear of fire, shipwreck, and typhus.

The crossing took 30 days.[20] After their ship sailed through the Narrows and entered Upper New York Bay, it headed directly for the East River and the seaport at South Street - the shipping capital of the New World in the first half of the 19th Century. The record reflects that on September 4th, a port official boarded the ship to collect the customs passenger list from Captain Sweetser and a health inspector boarded to quickly look for signs of typhus or other contagious diseases among the passengers. Apparently, all the paperwork must have been in order and the

---

[17]Laxton, 25.

[18]Laxton, 30.

[19]Laxton, 31.

[20]Maritime Intelligence, "Port of New York, September 5, 1849," *New York Herald*, Sunday, September 9, 1849, p. 4.

Arrived,
Bark Wm M. Chase (of Portland), Sweetser, Londonderry
30 days, with pig iron, to Perkins & Delano. Aug 25, on the
Grand Banks, spoke Br bark Rectitude, 22 days from Liverpool for Nova Scotia.

family must have passed muster as they were allowed to disembark despite what must have been their bedraggled appearance due to the rigors of a long voyage.

ARRIVING IN AMERICA

There is no record of who may have met the McCauley family in New York or how they made their way to Philadelphia. Depending on their financial resources, ingenuity, or instructions received by letter from family members they were joining in Philadelphia, it's possible they could have taken a stage, a train, or a coastal steamer or any combination of these for their journey from New York to Philadelphia. At a minimum, they probably walked about a half mile down South Street to the Battery where they would have initially booked passage on a steamer bound for the port city of Perth Amboy in New Jersey. Once there, they may have boarded a train operated by the Camden and Amboy Railroad for the trip south across the State of New Jersey to the city of Camden. Upon entering Camden, the train would have taken them directly down Bridge Avenue to the Camden and Amboy Railroad Ferry for the trip across the Delaware River to Philadelphia, their new home.[21]

All that can be said for certain is that the crowds at the South Street Seaport in New York must have been bustling at a frenetic pace. As the family came down the gangway, they would have seen the stevedores unloading the cargo from the ship onto the pier. Exiting from the wharf, the family must have walked cautiously, but deliberately, along the main cobblestoned thoroughfare of the seaport at South Street, fending off swindlers, marauders, robbers and even wild pigs. Although leaving their ship behind must have been an immense relief to all of them, they must have been equally amazed and bewildered by their new surroundings.

LIFE IN PHILADELPHIA

When the McCauley family arrived in Philadelphia in September of 1849, eager to begin their new life, they joined 400,000 people already in residence. Many of them were foreign-born immigrants such as themselves. Zachary Taylor was President of the United States, gold had been discovered in California, and the slavery controversy was again dogging the county. Closer to home, they discovered rather quickly that even though Philadelphia was a modern city in many respects, life was tough for most people. In fact, the city had just gone through a cholera epidemic earlier that year in which over a thousand people had died in the city and county of Philadelphia between May 30 and September 8, 1849.[22]

Nevertheless, large fortunes were being amassed by some Philadelphians. Business and industry was booming. Stately brick homes outfitted with many conveniences were being built

---

[21]Scharf and Westcott, *History of Philadelphia: 1609-1884*, 3 volumes (Philadelphia, Pennsylvania: Everts and Company, 1884), 2183.

[22]Scharf and Westcott, 690.

by the rich. Gas light was being used for illumination and coal for fuel. The Fairmount Waterworks was in operation having supplanted the pump and the well. Police service had taken the place of the nightwatch. The volunteer fire department was in all its glory, its large membership making it a powerful force in city politics. Society, in the narrowest sense of the word, placed great emphasis on wealth and indulged itself in fancy dress, the theater, and dancing.

The McCauley family was certainly not among the rich. In fact, they may not even have been solidly among the middle class. The 1850 census shows that Stephen and Margaret (Wallace) McCauley lived in a rented house near the intersection of Schuylkill 4th (later known as 19th Street) and Lombard Street in the section of the city known as Cedar Ward.[23,24] They shared the house with two other families - Ann Regan and her two young sons and Martin and Margaret Gregg and their two children. Margaret (Wallace) McCauley kept house while Stephen McCauley worked as a day laborer. Their next door neighbors were James and Bridget Brady who owned the grocery store on the corner.

Life was relatively quiet in Philadelphia for the McCauley family until September 3, 1850, when a violent storm hit the city.[25] Although losses from the storm were never completely ascertained, the area immediately adjacent to the Schuylkill, on both sides of the river, was extensively damaged. The bridge at Flat Rock was destroyed. The new bridge at the Falls of the Schuylkill was almost completely swept away with the exception of one arch. The water was ten and a half feet above its normal level at the Fairmount dam and, on the west side of the Schuylkill, near the Suspension Bridge, the water rose to 20 inches above the first floor of Harding's Tavern. William Street (later known as 24th Street) from Callowhill to Vine was flooded with the water extending nearly to Schuylkill Front (later known as 22nd Street). The gasworks was flooded halting the manufacture of gas and leaving the city in darkness. Candles were the only means of illumination in many homes. Even the street lamps in Philadelphia were dark until about 9 o'clock when tallow candles were placed in some of them. Large quantities of coal, wood and lumber were swept away from the wharves and on the western side of the Schuylkill, the cars of the Philadelphia, Wilmington and Baltimore Railroad could no longer safely cross the river at Gray's Ferry.

---

[23]1850 U.S. Census (population), Pennsylvania, Philadelphia County, City of Philadelphia, Cedar Ward, page 32, lines 1-3, National Archives Microfilm Publication M432, Roll 812, Household of Stephen McCaulley (sic).

[24]1850 U.S. Census (population), Pennsylvania, Philadelphia County, City of Philadelphia, North Ward, page 245A, lines 28-42, National Archives Microfilm Publication M432, Roll 817, Household of Margaret McCalley (sic). Inconclusive, but possible duplicate listing.

[25]Scharf and Westcott, 697.

It's impossible to know for certain, but the McCauley family's rented house may have escaped any great damage from the flooding as they were located about six blocks south of Market Street and five blocks east of the river. At a minimum, they would have had no gas light for a while. How the storm affected Stephen McCauley's job as a day-laborer is also unknown because there is no information about where he may have worked. In any event, the 1855 Philadelphia City Directory lists their address as Lombard, west of 19th Street, which may, in fact, have been the same house where they were living in 1850 or just around the corner.

Both Stephen and Margaret (Wallace) McCauley were quiet, conservative and God-fearing people. They had little, if any, formal education. Neither could read or write. They regularly attended the Presbyterian church. They didn't drink alcohol. Undoubtedly, Stephen McCauley belonged to at least one fraternal organization if for nothing else than the death insurance benefits. Their family circle was small, but included their cousins, the Wallaces and the Pattons.

In addition to their son, James McCauley, they had two more children. Thomas McCauley was born on February 14, 1854. His birth was followed by the winter of 1854/55 which was one of more than ordinary severity.[26] In addition to the harsh winter weather, many families in Philadelphia were also adversely affected by the scarcity of employment. The situation was so serious in terms of suffering and destitution that early in 1855, the city government set aside a relief appropriation for the poor and the soup-houses and various charitable organizations banded together to help people get through the winter.

Margaret McCauley was probably born on December 10, 1856.[27] She was born after another terrible winter (1855/56) which was for many years vivid in the minds of those who had lived through it.[28] It was so cold that the Delaware River froze solid from bank to bank as far south as the Horseshoe Channel. The city was, in effect, ice-bound. The economic losses to all segments of society in the city were so great that a meeting of concerned businessmen was held in February to devise a plan to reopen the river by using gunpowder to blow up the ice. Unfortunately, a test of the proposal was a complete failure and the citizens of Philadelphia, rich and poor alike, continued to suffer while the lone city ice-boat continued its losing battle to keep a channel of navigation open. It was not until March that the ice had broken up sufficiently to enable the ships that had been unable to reach the city to make some progress up the Delaware

---

[26]Scharf and Westcott, 716.

[27]Pennsylvania, Death Certificates, 1906-1964, Pennsylvania Historic and Museum Commission, Harrisburg, Pennsylvania, re: Margaret Wright, November 4, 1939, Philadelphia, Philadelphia County, Pennsylvania, <<www.ancestry.com>>, downloaded July 29, 2018, says Margaret (McCauley) Wright was born December 10, 1860 (sic), which was almost a year after the death of her mother.

[28]Scharf and Westcott, 720.

River.

In 1857, the year after Margaret McCauley was born, a financial panic was triggered in the city by the closing of the Bank of Philadelphia.[29] Businessmen were thrown into panic and some banks were forced to call the police to protect them from their creditors. The panic quickly spread through all segments of society followed by a great depression in trade and industry. Before the middle of October, there was little work to be had by laborers in the mills and factories. The streets were full of unemployed men. There were many meetings of tradesmen, workingmen and philanthropists during this period for the purpose of devising a scheme to relieve the distress of the poor. Some wealthy citizens even resorted to distributing bread directly to the people who needed it. Despite a mild winter and the charity of the wealthy, the suffering of the lower classes was widespread.

The McCauley family persevered through all these years - ten very hard years. Work was scarce for Stephen McCauley, but somehow he managed to find enough employment that his family survived intact. They maintained their faith. And, even though the city was hot in the summer and cold in the winter, and the children didn't attended the public school with any regularity, the future never looked better for the McCauleys than it did as the decade drew to a close.

GOODBYE LOVING MOM

Then, on January 3, 1860, tragedy struck and Margaret (Wallace) McCauley died. She was only 37 years old. The official record of her death reads simply:

January 3, 1860

Died this day of Typhoid Fever, Margaret Wallace, wife of
Stephen McCaulley (sic) (white) aged 37 years -

J.F. Gayley, M.D
133 South 18th Street[30]

How Margaret (Wallace) McCauley contracted typhoid fever is unknown. She may have been helping care for a friend or relative or she may have inadvertently drunk water or eaten food contaminated by a carrier. In any case, she soon would have noticed she had a headache and was running a low grade fever. No doubt, she tried to ignore the symptoms while going about her daily activities, but the fever would not go away. By the end of the week, it would have been

---

[29]Scharf and Westcott, 726.

[30]Doctor's Report of the Death of Margaret Wallace McCauley and Cemetery Return for Mount Moriah Cemetery for the Week Ending January 7, 1860, City of Philadelphia Archives, Philadelphia, Pensylvania.

unremitting rising to 104 degrees Fahrenheit in the evening. Soon she would have developed chills and been confined to her bed with increasing abdominal pain so bad she couldn't clean, cook or take care of the children. By the third week, she would have been delirious and so weak from the ravages of persistent fever and diarrhea that the doctor was summoned. There was nothing he could do to save her. The typhoid bacilli having perforated her intestines she was probably hemorrhaging. She likely had pneumonia. She probably died of acute circulatory failure. The irony of her death is that having escaped the famine in Ireland and enduring the hardships of the Atlantic crossing, she should die so young of typhoid fever thousands of miles from her birthplace in a city where opportunity was said to be endless.

Stephen McCauley bought a plot at Mount Moriah Cemetery in West Philadelphia where Margaret (Wallace) McCauley was laid to rest.[31,32] Notice of her death was placed in the *Philadelphia Public Ledger* on Wednesday, January 4, 1860.[33] Her funeral was held at 9 A.M. on January 5, 1860, at her late residence, 1728 South Street. There is very little other information available about her funeral except for a brief notation on her death record which says: *no carriages*. Stephen McCauley must have rented a wagon to transport her body to the cemetery as Mount Moriah is across the Schuylkill River, 3 miles from the foot of the Market Street bridge. It must have been a long, slow, cold and dreary journey for the family. It probably would have taken them all day to escort the body to the cemetery, attend the burial and return home. They would have arrived home late that evening, exhausted.

HE WAS HIS KIDS' DAD

Stephen McCauley never remarried. Instead, he put all his energy into working and raising his children, which he did with the help of his sister-in-law, Nancy Wallace, later known as Nancy (Wallace) Patton, who lived next door.[34] As far as can be determined, Stephen

---

[31]Letter dated January 26, 1996, from Mount Moriah Cemetery stating Margaret (Wallace) McCauley was buried in Section 16, Lot 105 on January 4, 1860.

[32]Burial of Margaret McCauley, Record ID 36132, Mount Moriah Cemetery Database, Genealogical Society of Pennsylvania, Philadelphia, Pennsylvania, <<genpa.org>>, downloaded July 30, 2018.

[33]Obituary of Margaret McCauley, *Philadelphia Public Ledger*, Wednesday, January 4, 1860, p 2, Library of Congress, Washington, D.C.

> On the 3rd inst., Mrs. MARGARET MCCAULEY, wife of Stephen McCauley, aged 37 years. The relatives and friends of the family are respectfully invited to attend the funeral, from her late residence, No. 1728 South st., on Thursday morning next at 9 o'clock - to proceed to Mount Moriah Cemetery.

[34]1860 U.S. Census (population), Pennsylvania, Philadelphia County, City of Philadelphia, Ward 1, page 598, lines 24-27 & 32-34, National Archives Microfilm Publication

McCauley was a good father even though he did not place an emphasis on the need for formal education for his children. As a widower, he did the best he could to raise his children properly under the most difficult circumstances. He provided for their religious education. He did not send them to live with relatives nor did he place them in institutional care. He did not strike out for California during the gold rush nor did he serve in the Civil War. By all accounts, he always provided for them from his daily labor.

TABOR PRESBYTERIAN CHURCH

The McCauley family regularly attended the Presbyterian church. Unfortunately, there is no known record of the church Stephen and Margaret (Wallace) McCauley attended when they first arrived in Philadelphia. They may have attended the Second Associate Reformed Presbyterian Church located at 19th and Lombard Streets as that congregation was organized in 1844 and the church was located in the same block in which they lived.

In any case, by 1857, the Philadelphia Sabbath-School Association started a Sabbath-school on Monroe Street between Seventeenth and Eighteenth Streets.[35] This also was near where the McCauley family lived and it is likely that Stephen McCauley took the children to this Sabbath School after his wife died. In fact, James, Thomas, and Margaret McCauley all probably attended the Sabbath-school regularly under the watchful eye of their father from the time they were very young children.

Membership grew rapidly and soon the Sabbath-school was relocated to larger quarters at 17th and Catherine Streets. There it was taken under the care of the Calvary Presbyterian Church where it became known as the Tabor Chapel. In April 1863, Tabor Chapel was organized as the Tabor Presbyterian Church. The Reverend Robert Adair was the first pastor. In 1871, Tabor Presbyterian Church relocated to a new building at 18th and Christian Streets where it stood for 60 years as a leading congregation in South Philadelphia.

According to family legend, the McCauley family attended Tabor Presbyterian Church from the time it was founded in 1863 until well after they moved to their new home in West Philadelphia in 1912. The session minutes reveal that Thomas McCauley formally joined Tabor Presbyterian Church on October 20, 1878 when he was 24 years old. This church was so important to the lives of the McCauley family that Thomas McCauley named his youngest son, Willis Skillman McCauley, in honor of its second pastor, the Reverend Willis B. Skillman.

M653, Roll 1151, Household of Stephen McCauley and Household of Anthony Romes (sic).

[35]Kenneth A. Hammonds, *Historical Directory of Presbyterian Churches and Presbyteries of Greater Philadelphia Related to the Presbyterian Church (USA) and Its Antecedents 1690-1990*, (Philadelphia, Pennsylvania: Presbyterian Historical Society, 1993), 60.

BRICKS, BRICKS, BRICKS

In 1870, Stephen McCauley was still working as a laborer.[36,37,38] His daughter, Margaret McCauley, was cooking and keeping house for the family and her brothers, James and Thomas McCauley, were contributing substantially to the family income by having learned the brickmaking trade. It was a good move on their part as work was readily available within walking distance of their house for anyone skilled in brickmaking.

Brick was extensively employed in building the city of Philadelphia beginning as early as 1684. For that reason, there were always a great number of mills, brick-kilns, and tile-ovens in the area. According to Jonathan Dickinson (in the Logan Papers), the kilns in Philadelphia furnished "a considerable quantity of the best bricks on the continent, ... which prompts people to make substantial buildings, both in brick and stone. We have been upon regulating the pavements of our streets - the footways with brick and the cartways with stone - and this, with buildings, have made bricks so scarce that the inhabitants would go to the kilns, and there strive [to purchase] them at 28 per mill; that is and will be the price here." This being the case, at the close of the 18th century, four-fifths of the buildings in the city were made of brick, and the reputation of the kilns was very high for the beauty and durability of the bricks.[39]

By 1857, there were fifty brick-making establishments in the city that annually produced one hundred million common bricks and eight million fine pressed bricks.[40] In South Philadelphia, the section of the city where the McCauleys lived, there were more than half a dozen brickmaking establishments. Arrison & Dingee operated an establishment at Washington and 23rd Streets. The Gillespie kiln and the kiln of Peter Bobb were both located at Federal near Gray's Ferry. Charles W. Carns' establishment was located at 23rd and Federal Streets and James Harper's kiln was at 19th near Carpenter Street. There were other kilns located in the immediate vicinity and exactly where the McCauley brothers worked is not known.

---

[36]1870 U.S. Census (population), 1st enumeration, Pennsylvania, Philadelphia County, City of Philadelphia, Ward 26, Election District 86, page 347B, lines 34-37, National Archives Microfilm Publication M593, Roll 1414, Households of Maurice (sic) Patton and Steven McCauley.

[37]1870 U.S. Census (population), 2nd enumeration, Pennsylvania, Philadelphia County, City of Philadelphia, Ward 26, Election District 86, page 151B, lines 32-36, National Archives Microfilm Publication M593, Roll 1441, Households of Nancy Patton and James McCally (sic).

[38]1870 Philadelphia city directory.

[39]Scharf and Westcott, p. 2293.

[40]Scharf and Westcott, p. 2293.

Neither do we know the type of brick the brothers manufactured nor the method of brickmaking they employed. Most likely, however, James and Thomas McCauley made common bricks as these were the most widely manufactured bricks in Philadelphia. Common bricks vary in color from a dark orange to yellow or deep red, depending on the type of clay used. *Bricks can be made by a stiff-mud process or a dry-press process.* As most bricks produced in the United States today are made by the stiff-mud process, this is probably the method of brickmaking used at the establishments where the McCauley brothers worked. In this process, James and Thomas McCauley would have been responsible for pressing a mixtures of wet surface clays and shales into molds before the bricks were fired. A messy process in contrast to the dry-press method which uses high pressure to compress a fairly dry clay in a mold.

With respect to the method of brickmaking they employed, it is entirely possible that the establishment where the McCauley brothers worked could have used modern kilns by the standards of the mid- to late-19th century. Modern kilns were permanent enclosures where the heat was generated by external ovens. The heated air was circulated through the bricks which were stacked in the kiln to produce a fairly uniform masonry unit.

Modern kilns are of two types - intermittent and continuous - and, eventhough it is not known what type of kiln was used where James and Thomas McCauley were employed, they probably worked in an intermittent kiln where they piled, fired, and cooled the bricks and then removed them from the kiln before they piled in the new bricks to be fired. Bricks made in intermittent kilns in Philadelphia were usually burned in clamps containing from 40,000 to 50,000 bricks at a time, consuming half a cord of wood, and taking a week to burn.[41]

If the brothers happened to work at a continuous (or tunnel) kiln, which is less likely, they would have loaded the moist clay on special cars that were drawn through the kiln at a constant rate of speed. As the clay passed through the tunnel, which consisted of several zones in which the temperature was carefully controlled, it was successively shaped, dried, fired, and cooled to produce a uniform product. Either way, it was hard work.

BECOMING A CITIZEN

The record indicates that Stephen McCauley, a native of Ireland, first appeared before the Prothonotary of the District Court for the City and County of Philadelphia on November 5, 1861, to renounce his allegiance to the Queen of Great Britain and Ireland and file his declaration of intent to become a citizen of the United States.[42] He claimed to be 30 years old in his declaration of intent, but it is unclear whether he was referring to his age when he came to the United States

---

[41]Scharf and Westcott, p. 2293.

[42]Declaration of Intent of Stephen McCaulley (sic), District Court for the City and County of Philadelphia, November 5, 1861, City of Philadelphia Archives, Philadelphia, Pennsylvania.

in 1849 or his present age which would have been about 40.

For some reason, Stephen McCauley never pursued filing a petition for naturalization until 1868. He probably did not complete the naturalization process earlier because, at that time, American citizenship conferred little more than the right to vote and Stephen McCauley may have been too busy earning a living to worry about voting.

In any event, in 1868, the Pennsylvania legislature passed a law that, henceforth, men of foreign birth would be required to present their Naturalization Certificate as proof of citizenship before they were allowed to vote. The election of 1868 must have been contentious as it appears to have provided Stephen McCauley with the incentive he needed to complete the naturalization process. Thus, he was naturalized on September 21, 1868, just in time to vote in the National election wherein General U.S. Grant was elected to the Presidency.[43] Interestingly, Stephen McCauley's witness at his naturalization proceeding was one Thomas Wallace, a citizen of the United States.

His son, James McCauley, was not naturalized separately because he arrived in the United States with his parents in 1849 as an infant and he was under 21 years of age in 1868 when his father was naturalized. Thus, under a provision of the naturalization laws then in effect in the United States, James McCauley was automatically naturalized by his father's naturalization.[44]

THE PATTONS

Sometime between 1860 and 1870, the McCauley family moved a few blocks east to 1017 Ward Street where they shared a house with the Patton family.[45,46] Thus began a long association of the McCauley family (including their descendants, the Wrights and the Mullers)

---

[43]Petition for Naturalization of Stephen McCaulley (sic), District Court for the City and County of Philadelphia, September 21, 1868, City of Philadelphia Archives, Philadelphia, Pennsylvania.

[44]Arlene Eakle and Johni Cerny, *The Source - A Guidebook of American Genealogy*, (Salt Lake City, Utah: Ancestry, Inc., 1984), 470.

[45]1870 U.S. Census (population), 1st enumeration, Pennsylvania, Philadelphia County, City of Philadelphia, Ward 26, Election District 86, page 347B, lines 34-37, National Archives Microfilm Publication M593, Roll 1414, Households of Maurice (sic) Patton and Steven McCauley.

[46]1870 U.S. Census (population), 2nd enumeration, Pennsylvania, Philadelphia County, City of Philadelphia, Ward 26, Election District 86, page 151B, lines 32-36, National Archives Microfilm Publication M593, Roll 1441, Households of Nancy Patton and James McCally (sic).

with the Patton family that lasted over 50 years ending only with the death of William Wallace Patton. His mother, Nancy (Wallace) Patton, was Stephen McCauley's sister-in-law and the beloved aunt of his children, James, Thomas, and Margaret McCauley.

Before she was married, Nancy (Wallace) Patton lived next door to the McCauley family and, undoubtedly, helped Stephen McCauley with the children after the death of his wife (and her sister).[47] She married William Patton, (Sr.), a shoemaker, on December 18, 1860 at Westminster Presbyterian Church.[48]

After their marriage, William Patton, (Sr.), was listed in the 1861 city directory living at 1737 South Street and in the 1863 city directory living at 1017 Ward Street. Their first child, Thomas Patton, was born at 1017 Ward Street on July 2, 1862.[49] Unfortunately, the child lived only 36 hours. He was buried in Mount Moriah Cemetery.[50] Their second child, William Wallace Patton, was also born at 1017 Ward Street on January 21, 1866.[51] Unfortunately, he never knew his father.

William Patton, (Sr.), died on October 13, 1866, and was buried at Mount Moriah Cemetery.[52] His obituary appeared in the *Philadelphia Public Ledger*. It read as follows:

---

[47]1860 U.S. Census (population), Pennsylvania, Philadelphia County, City of Philadelphia, Ward 1, page 598, lines 24-27 & 32-34, National Archives Microfilm Publication M653, Roll 1151, Household of Stephen McCauley and Household of Anthony Romes (sic).

[48]Westminster United (sic) Presbyterian Church, Session Minutes 1853-1900, Philadelphia, Pennsylvania, FHL Microfilm Roll 913506, Item 4.

[49]Pennsylvania, Philadelphia City Births, 1860-1906, FHL Microfilm Roll 1289307, <<www.familysearch.org>>, downloaded August 14, 2018, re: Thomas Patton, b. July 2, 1866; Book 1866 p. 7. Note: Mother's name was listed as Ann. His mother was known as Nancy which was originally a diminutive form of the name Ann.

[50]Pennsylvania, Philadelphia City Death Certificates, 1803-1915, FHL Microfilm Roll 1977751, <<www.familysearch.org>>, downloaded August 14, 2018, re: Thomas Patton, d. July 4, 1862, Mount Moriah Cemetery.

[51]Pennsylvania, Philadelphia City Births, 1860-1906, FHL Microfilm Roll 1289310, <<www.familysearch.org>>, downloaded August 14, 2018, re: William Wallace Patton, b. January 21, 1866; Book 1866 p. 7. Note: Mother's name was listed as Ann. His mother was known as Nancy which was originally a diminutive form of the name Ann.

[52]Pennsylvania, Philadelphia City Death Certificates, 1803-1915, FHL Microfilm Roll 1987620, <<www.familysearch.org>>, downloaded August 14, 2018, re: William Patton, d. October 13, 1866, Mount Moriah Cemetery.

> PATTON - On the 13th, instant., William Patton, in the 45th year of his age.
> The relatives and friends of the family, and members of Philadelphia Lodge,
> No. 50 American Protestant Association, are respectfully invited to attend
> his funeral from his late residence No. 1017 Ward Street, on Monday, the
> 15th, instant., at 2½ o'clock.[53]

Thereafter, Nancy (Wallace) Patton was listed in the Philadelphia city directory as the widow of William Patton.[54] Almost all of her energy was devoted to raising her son. She never remarried. She was a very active and respected member of Tabor Presbyterian Church having joined on April 4, 1879.[55] She died October 20, 1893.[56] Special mention was made of her passing in the Session Minutes of the church.[57] She was buried in the McCauley family plot at Mount Moriah Cemetery alongside her husband, her son, Thomas, and her sister, Margaret (Wallace) McCauley, Stephen McCauley's wife.

The obituary of Nancy (Wallace) Patton appeared in the *Philadelphia Public Ledger* on Saturday, October 21, 1893. It read as follows:

> PATTON, On the 20th inst., Nancy, widow of the late William Patton. The
> relatives and friends and Liberty Lodge No 3 of the A.P.L.A. are respectfully
> invited to attend her funeral from her late residence on No. 1017 Ward Street on
> Monday at 2 o'clock. Interment Mount Moriah.[58]

Her only surviving son, William Wallace Patton, continued to live with members of the McCauley family (including the Wrights and the Mullers) throughout much of his life including his two marriages - first to Mary Rutherford Dunbar whom he married on October 22, 1890 at the Church of the Holy Apostles (Episcopal) and from whom he was divorced on March 6, 1893; and

---

[53]Obituary of William Patton, *Philadelphia Public Ledger*, Monday, October 15. 1866, Philadelphia, Pennsylvania, <<www.genealogybank.com>>, downloaded August 14, 2018.

[54]1869 Philadelphia city directory.

[55]Tabor Presbyterian Church, Session Minutes, Volume I, April 4, 1879, page 171, Presbyterian Historical Society, Philadelphia, Pennsylvania.

[56]Pennsylvania, Philadelphia City Death Certificates, 1803-1915, FHL Microfilm Roll 1987620, <<www.familysearch.org>>, downloaded August 14, 2018, re: Nancy Patton, d. October 20, 1893, Mount Moriah Cemetery.

[57]Tabor Presbyterian Church, Session Minutes, Volume II, November 21, 1893, p 142, Presbyterian Historical Society, Philadelphia, Pennsylvania.

[58]Obituary of Nancy Patton, *Philadelphia Public Ledger*, Saturday, October 21, 1893, p 8, Library of Congress, Washington, D.C.

second to Ella Stewart whom he married on June 2, 1902, at Tabor Presbyterian Church.[59,60]

In fact, the only time William Wallace Patton can be found living apart from the McCauleys, the Wrights or the Mullers was in 1908 when Robert Wright, the husband of Margaret (McCauley) Wright, died at 1025 Dorrance Street and in 1910 when Margaret (McCauley) Wright, widow of Robert Wright, and her two teenaged daughters, Margaret Ann Wright and Agnes Wallace Wright, were enumerated at 924 South 18th Street.[61,62] Both addresses were only about a block from 1017 S. Cleveland Street (formerly known as 1017 Ward Street), the residence of William Wallace Patten.[63]

On December 10, 1913, while still living at 1017 S. Cleveland Street, William Wallace Patton bought a plot at Mount Moriah Cemetery.[64] On August 24, 1914, he moved his mother, Nancy (Wallace) Patton, his father, William Patton, (Sr.), and his brother, Thomas Patton, to the new plot.

---

[59]Pennsylvania, Philadelphia Marriage Records, 1885-1951, FHL Microfilm Roll 1299858, <<www.familysearch.org>>, downloaded August 14, 2018, re: Affidavit of Applicant for Marriage License # 37876, October 11, 1890 (William Patton & Mary R. Dunbar). Married October 22, 1890 by Rev. Charles D. Cooper, Church of the Holy Apostles (Episcopal), 21st & Christian.

[60]Pennsylvania, Philadelphia Marriage Records, 1885-1951, FHL Microfilm Roll 1276696, <<www.familysearch.org>>, downloaded August 14, 2018, re: Affidavit of Applicant for Marriage License # 148315, May 31, 1902 (William Patton & Ellie Stewart). Married June 2, 1902, by Rev. Willis B. Skillman, Tabor Presbyterian Church, 18th & Christian.

[61]Pennsylvania Death Certificates,1906-1966, Death Certificate of Rob Wright, January 11, 1908, Philadelphia, Philadelphia County, Pennsylvania, <<www.ancestry.com>>, downloaded August 15, 2018.

[62]1910 U.S. Census (population), Pennsylvania, Philadelphia County, City of Philadelphia, Ward 30, E.D. 0701, Family Number 0085, page 4B, lines 57-59, National Archives Microfilm T624, Roll 1400, Household of Margaret Wright.

[63]1910 U.S. Census (population), Pennsylvania, Philadelphia County, City of Philadelphia, Ward 30, E.D. 0701, Family Number 0094, page 4B, lines 94-95, National Archives Microfilm T624, Roll 1400, Household of William Patton.

[64]Mount Moriah Cemetery Association, Deed 116, Registered in Book B, page 46, Lot Numbered 5 Middle Part of East Part, Range 3, original deed in the possession of Kathryn C. Torpey, 5035 Domain Place, Alexandria, Virginia 22311. Note: The address on the deed indicated for William Patton was 1017 S. Cleveland Avenue (sic).

After living apart from his cousins for a few years, William Wallace Patton and his wife, Ella (Stewart) Patton, moved to 1956 S. Ithan Street where they lived out the rest of their lives in the home of his cousin, Margaret (Wright) Muller and her family.[65] When Ella (Stewart) Patton died at Presbyterian Hospital on July 1, 1919, the informant was her husband, William Patton of 1956 S. Ithan Street.[66] When William Patton died at the Home for Incurables on March 11, 1921, the informant was his first cousin (once removed), Margaret McCauley who lived at 1606 S. 53rd Street, about 3 blocks from the Mullers and the Pattons.[67] On July 5, 1919, and on March 15, 1921, respectively, Ella (Stewart) Patton and William Wallace Patton were buried in the Patton family plot at Mount Moriah Cemetery.[68,69] As far as is known, William Wallace Patton had no children.

William Wallace Patton left behind a double-barreled, 12-gauge shotgun that eventually came into the possession of Henry Grafe Chambers, the husband of Mary Ann (McCauley) Chambers. Henry Grafe Chambers used the shotgun when he and August Muller went rabbit and duck hunting in the years preceding World War II.[70]

---

[65]1920 U.S. Census (population), Pennsylvania, Philadelphia County, City of Philadelphia, Ward 40, E.D. 1498, page 4A, lines 31-43, National Archives Microfilm T625, Roll 1641, Household of August C. Muller.

[66]Pennsylvania Death Certificates,1906-1966, Death Certificate of Ella Stewart Patton, July 1, 1919, Presbyterian Hospital, Philadelphia, Philadelphia County, Pennsylvania, <<www.ancestry.com>>, downloaded August 15, 2018.

[67]Pennsylvania Death Certificates,1906-1966, Death Certificate of William Patton, March 1, 1921, Home for Incurables, Philadelphia, Philadelphia County, Pennsylvania, <<www.ancestry.com>>, downloaded August 15, 2018.

[68]Obituary of Ella Stewart Patton, *Philadelphia Inquirer*, Thursday, July 3, 1919, <<www.genealogybank.com>>, downloaded August 16, 2018.

> PATTON - July 1, ELLA STEWART, wife of William Patton. Relatives and friends invited to service, Sat., 2 P.M., residence, 1956 S. Ithan st. Int. Mt Moriah Cem.

[69]Obituary of William Patton, *Philadelphia Inquirer*, Saturday, March 12, 1921, <<www.genealogybank.com>>, downloaded August 16, 2018.

> PATTON - March 11, WILLIAM, husband of late Ella Stuart (sic) Patton. Relatives and friends, also all organizations of which he was a member, are invited to service, Tues. 2 P.M., at the Oliver Bair Bldg., 1820 Chestnut st. Int. Mt. Moriah Cem. Friends may call Mon. eve.

[70]The shotgun was in the possession of the late William Scott Chambers, 325 NW 95th Avenue, Plantation, Florida 33324.

AMERICAN PROTESTANT ASSOCIATION

According to family legend, the McCauley family was associated with the American Protestant Association. In fact, the obituary of William Patton, (Sr.), mentions that he was a member of Philadelphia Lodge No. 50 of the American Protestant Association and Nancy (Wallace) Patton's obituary mentions that she was a member of Liberty Lodge No. 3 of the A.P.L.A, possibly a ladies auxiliary connected to same group.

The American Protestant Association with which the McCauley family was said to be affiliated is described variously as the oldest American, exclusively anti-Roman Catholic, secret society in the United States and a prototype of the American Protective Association.[71] According to a former chief executive of the American Protestant Association:

> It was not the Orange Institution and there is no affiliation between them. There is nothing on record as to what was the cause for forming the "A.P.A.," but I have always understood that at that time there was no Protestant society to which citizens of foreign birth could be admitted that had for its fundamental principles the maintenance of civil and religious liberty, and the maintenance of the Bible in our public schools; hence the "A.P.A.," to which all Protestants of good moral character may be admitted.[72]

Although it was a secret society with ritual and degrees, its emphasis was apparently more patriotic than fraternal. At its highest point, there were at least 200,000 members of the American Protestant Association. After 1900, the society began to decline. Although it still existed as late as the early 1920s, as far as can be determined, it no longer exists today.[73]

DOCTOR THOMAS HARRISON MOONEY

According to family legend, Doctor Thomas Harrison Mooney was a "shirt-tail

---

[71]Albert C. Stevens, *The Cyclopedia of Fraternities - A Compilation of Existing Authentic Information and the Results of Original Investigations as to the Origin, Derivation, Founders, Development Aims, Emblems, Character, and Personnel of More Than Six Hundred Secret Societies in the United States* (New York: Hamilton Printing and Publishing Company, 1899), p. 298.

[72]Stevens, p 298.

[73]Alvin J. Schmidt, *Fraternal Organizations* (Westport, Connecticut: Greenwood Press, 1980), 38.

relative."[74] He is also said to have been the McCauley family doctor.[75] Born on July 27, 1888, in Philadelphia, he was the son of John Mooney and Eliza Jane Boyd. His maternal grandparents were Robert Boyd and Grace Kelly who were married on February 10, 1849, in Coleraine, County Coleraine, aka County Londonderry, Ireland.[76,77] The records of the American Medical Association state:

> Mooney, Thomas Harrison, ⊗ Rosemont, Pa; *Medico-Chirurgical College of Philadelphia*, 1912; died Oct 25, aged 79, of cerebrovascular accident.[78]

CHILDREN OF STEPHEN AND MARGARET (WALLACE) MCCAULEY

James, We Hardly Knew You

Stephen and Margaret (Wallace) McCauley's oldest son, James McCauley, was just a baby when he arrived in Philadelphia in 1849 and he was only 40 years old when he died on June 4, 1889.[79] He was buried on June 6, 1889, alongside his mother at Mount Moriah Cemetery.[80] In

---

[74]Commonly, someone who is a relative by marriage or is only distantly related, such as a fourth cousin, or is a family friend with honorary status as a relative.

[75]Email dated August 11, 1998, from the late William Scott Chamber, 325 N.W. 95th Avenue, Plantation, Florida 33324-7021, stating, in part, "I forgot to mention Dr. Mooney. My mother [Mary Ann (McCauley) Chambers] and Aunt Marge [Margaret (McCauley) Smith] were patients of the good doctor ... ."

[76]Pennsylvania Death Certificates,1906-1966, Death Certificate of Eliza Jane Mooney, November 24, 1914, Philadelphia, Philadelphia County, Pennsylvania, <<www.ancestry.com>>, downloaded August 19, 2018.

[77]Ireland Civil Registration, 1845-1913, Robert Boyd and Grace Ann Kelly, Marriage February 10, 1849, Coleraine, County Coleraine, Ireland; General Register Office, Dublin; FHL Microfilm Roll 101305, <<www.familysearch.org>>, downloaded August 19, 2018. Note: Robert Boyd's father was Thomas Boyd and Grace Ann Kelly's father was James Kelly.

[78]*Journal of the American Medical Association*, Vol. 203, January 1968, p. 181.

[79]Pennsylvania, Philadelphia City Death Registers, 1803-1915, James McCauley, June 4, 1889; Volume 1, p. 239, FHL Microfilm Roll 1003715, <<www.familysearch.org>>, downloaded August 22, 2018

[80]Obituary of James McCauley, *Philadelphia Public Ledger*, Wednesday, June 5, 1889, p. 2, Library of Congress, Washington, D.C.

McCAULEY - On the 4th inst., James McCauley. Funeral on Thursday at 1

between, he grew up and made bricks. He always lived at home, principally at 1017 Ward Street.
He never married. Nothing more is known about him.

Margaret, Their Only Daughter

Stephen and Margaret McCauley's only daughter, Margaret "Maggie" (McCauley)
Wright, was always known as Granny to her grandchildren and Aunt Mamie to her nieces and
nephews. She did not have an easy life. Her mother died when she was only 4 years old. By the
time she was 14, she was keeping house for her father and brothers making it necessary for her to
drop out of school.

She married late, at about the age of 28. Her husband was Robert Wright, the son of
Hugh and Margaret (McCorkle) Wright. According to the *Wright Family Bible*, Robert Wright
was from Londonderry, Ireland, and they were married on April 27.[81] Unfortunately, neither the
year nor the place of their marriage was recorded in the *Wright Family Bible*. It does not appear
in the Philadelphia Marriage Registers possibly because their marriage took place in 1885, the
year the new reporting requirements went into effect or it took place outside Philadelphia.

Robert Wright moved to 1017 Ward Street after he and Margaret McCauley were married
where they shared the house with the Pattons and the McCauleys. At the time of their marriage,
Robert Wright belonged to Union Presbyterian Church which was then located in Center City
Philadelphia at 13th and Budd Streets. He was examined and admitted to membership in that
church by profession of faith on March 13, 1884.[82] Margaret (McCauley) Wright officially
transferred her membership from Tabor Presbyterian Church to Union Presbyterian Church on
December 14, 1886.[83] When they attended Sunday services, the Wright family always sat in pew
number 7 for which Robert Wright paid a pew rental fee of $2.00 per quarter.[84]

Robert Wright worked as a driver and teamster. He belonged to a fraternal organization
known as the Foresters of America whose primary objective was to provide sick and funeral

---

o'clock, from his late residence at 1017 Ward Street. Proceed to Mt. Moriah.

[81]*The Wright Family Bible - The New Illuminated Holy Bible*, (Philadelphia and New
York: American Bible House, 1807), is in the possession of Kathryn C. Torpey, 5035 Domain
Place, Alexandria, Virginia 22311.

[82]Session Minutes (1840-1898), Union Presbyterian Church, Philadelphia, Pennsylvania,
FHL Microfilm Roll 0525743.

[83]Session Minutes (1840-1898), Union Presbyterian Church, Philadelphia, Pennsylvania,
FHL Microfilm Roll 0525743.

[84]Pew Rents (1870-1897), Union Presbyterian Church, Philadelphia, Pennsylvania, FHL
Microfilm Roll 0525743.

benefits for members and those dependent upon them.[85] Membership was restricted to white men between the ages of eighteen and fifty who were of good moral character, of sound health and body, free from disease, and who believed in a Supreme Being.

Together, Robert and Margaret (McCauley) Wright had four children. Their oldest son, Robert "Robbie" Wright, Jr., was born in January 1888 and their second son, Thomas Wallace Wright, was born on April 10, 1890, just five days after the tragic death of his 18-month old first cousin, Thomas Wallace McCauley. In fact, given the unfortunate circumstances, Robert and Margaret (McCauley) Wright may have named their new baby boy after their recently departed nephew.

Thomas Wallace Wright was baptized at Union Presbyterian Church on December 18, 1890.[86] Unfortunately, he died shortly thereafter on February 12, 1891. His obituary in the *Philadelphia Public Ledger* read as follows:

> WRIGHT - On February 12, 1891, Thomas W., youngest son of Robert and Margaret Wright, aged 10 months, The relatives and friends of the family are respectfully invited to attend the funeral on Saturday afternoon at 2 o'clock from his parents' residence, 1017 Ward Street. To proceed to Mount Moriah Cemetery.[87]

Then, their oldest son, Robert "Robbie" Wright, died on February 13, 1893. His obituary appeared in the *Philadelphia Public Ledger* on February 14, 1893. It read as follows:

> WRIGHT - On the 13th inst., Robbie, son of Robert and Maggie Wright, aged 5 years and 1 month. Funeral services on Wednesday at 2 o'clock from the residence of his parents, 1017 Ward Street. Interment at Mount Moriah.[88]

Robert "Robbie" Wright and Thomas Wallace Wright were both buried in the Wright family plot at Mount Moriah Cemetery.[89] Their sisters, Margaret Ann Wright and Agnes

---

[85]Stevens, p. 126.

[86]Baptisms (1842-1891), Union Presbyterian Church, Philadelphia, Pennsylvania, FHL Microfilm Roll 0525743.

[87]Obituary of Thomas Wallace Wright, *Philadelphia Public Ledger*, Friday, February 13, 1891, p. 4, Library of Congress, Washington, D.C.

[88]Obituary of Robert Wright, *Philadelphia Public Ledger*, Tuesday, February 14, 1893, p. 4, Library of Congress, Washington, D.C.

[89]Letter dated June 2, 1997, from the late Marion Muller Wilson stating that Robert Wright, Jr., and Thomas Wallace Wright were buried at Mount Moriah Cemetery, in Section 146, Lot 10 belonging to Robert Wright, Sr.

Wallace Wright, were born on December 31, 1891, and November 14, 1893, respectively.[90,91]

Although Robert and Margaret (McCauley) Wright gave up their pew at Union Presbyterian Church in October 1891, they continued to attend that church until January 26, 1896, when they transferred to Tabor Presbyterian Church. Apparently, their transfer was in conjunction with the relocation of Union Presbyterian Church to 66th and Woodland Avenue in West Philadelphia.

As late as 1900, the Wright family was still living at 1017 Ward Street (known as 1017 S. Cleveland Street after 1897) with Margaret (McCauley) Wright's first cousin, William Patton. As their daughters got older, however, the family moved one block west to 1025 Dorrance Street. Sadly, tragedy struck again in 1908 when Robert Wright contracted pneumonia. He died at the age of 43 leaving Margaret (McCauley) Wright as the sole support for her two daughters who were 17 and 15 years old at the time of their father's death.[92]

His obituary appeared in the *Philadelphia Inquirer* on January 15, 1908. It read as follows:

> WRIGHT - On January 11, 1908, ROBERT, husband of Margaret Wright (nee McCauley), and son of the late Hugh and Margaret Wright. Relatives and friends, Court Caledonia No. 72, F of A, and employees of Carnwath & Bell, are invited to attend the funeral, on Wednesday, at 2 P.M. from his late residence, 1025 Dorrence st. Interment at Mount Moriah Cemetery.[93]

Notwithstanding the insurance benefits from the Foresters of America, Margaret (McCauley) Wright was forced to go to work to support her family. Capitalizing on all her years of housekeeping for her father and brothers, she initially went to work for the Bell Telephone Company as a cook. Soon, she became head cook and then she left the company to become the

---

[90]Pennsylvania, Philadelphia City Births, 1860-1906, FHL Microfilm Roll 1289331, <<www.familysearch.org>>, downloaded August 25, 2018, re: Margaret A. Wright, b. December 31, 1891, Father: Robt. Wright, Mother: Mgt. Wright, Book 1893, p. 371.

[91]Pennsylvania, Philadelphia City Births, 1860-1906, FHL Microfilm Roll 1289333, <<www.familysearch.org>>, downloaded August 25, 2018, re: Agnes W. Wright, b. November 14, 1893, Father: Robert Wright, Mother: Margaret, Book July 1893, p. 274.

[92]Pennsylvania Death Certificates,1906-1966, Death Certificate of Rob (sic) Wright, January 11, 1908, Philadelphia, Philadelphia County, Pennsylvania, <<www.ancestry.com>>, downloaded August 24, 2018.

[93]Obituary of Robert Wright, *Philadelphia Inquirer*, Wednesday, January 15, 1908, <<www.genealogybank.com>>, downloaded August 24, 2018.

cook for one of the families of the senior executives.[94] By 1910, she and the girls had moved to 924 South 18th Street where they shared a house with the family of David Renshaw.[95] To make ends meet, Margaret's daughters went to work, too. Although it is not known where Agnes Wallace Wright worked, Margaret (McCauley) Wright's oldest daughter, Margaret Ann Wright, worked at the Rump Leather Goods Company machining handbags.

Eventually, both of her daughters married and had families of their own. Agnes Wallace Wright was married to Earl Seitzinger Berger on February 7, 1913, in Wilmington, Delaware, by the Rev. George. L. Wolfe of the Methodist Protestant Church and Margaret Ann Wright was married to August Muller on May 28, 1917 in Philadelphia by the Rev. George F. Pentecost of Bethany Presbyterian Church.[96,97] Both families remained close to their cousins, the McCauleys and the Pattons. Initially, Margaret (McCauley) Wright went to live with her youngest daughter, Agnes Wallace (Wright) Berger, at 106 North Edgewood Street while William Patton and his second wife, Ella (Stewart) Patton, went to live with the Mullers at 1956 S. Ithan Street in West Philadelphia. In fact, Ella (Stewart) Patton died on July 1, 1919, while living with the Mullers as did William Patton on March 11, 1921.[98,99]

---

[94]E-mail dated October 8, 1998, from the late Marion Muller Wilson describing her grandmother's and her mother's occupation after the death of Robert Wright.

[95]1910 U.S. Census (population), Pennsylvania, Philadelphia County, City of Philadelphia, Ward 30, E.D. 0701, Family Number 0085, page 4B, lines 57-59, National Archives Microfilm T624, Roll 1400, Household of Margaret Wright.

[96]Delaware Marriage Records, 1806-1933, Register of Marriages, <www.ancestry.com>>, downloaded August 24, 2018, re: Earl Seitzinger Berger to Agnes W. Wright, February 7, 1913, New Castle County, Delaware.

[97]Affidavit of Applicant for Marriage License [with Return], # 36932, May 28, 1917, (August C. Muller & Margaret A. Wright), Philadelphia, Pennsylvania Civil Marriages, 1677-1950, <<www.familysearch.org>>, downloaded August 24, 2018.

[98]Obituary of Ella Stewart Patton, *Philadelphia Inquirer*, Thursday, July 3, 1919, <<www.genealogybank.com>>, downloaded August 16, 2018.

> PATTON - July 1, ELLA STEWART, wife of William Patton. Relatives and
> friends invited to service, Sat., 2 P.M., residence, 1956 S. Ithan st. Int. Mt
> Moriah Cem.

[99]Obituary of William Patton, *Philadelphia Inquirer*, Saturday, March 12, 1921, <<www.genealogybank.com>>, downloaded August 16, 2018.

> PATTON - March 11, WILLIAM, husband of late Ella Stuart (sic) Patton.
> Relatives and friends, also all organizations of which he was a member, are
> invited to service, Tues. 2 P.M., at the Oliver Bair Bldg., 1820 Chestnut st. Int.

After the death of her youngest daughter, Agnes Wallace (Wright) Berger, on November 21, 1934, Margaret (McCauley) Wright moved to Norwood in Delaware County, where she lived out the rest of her days with her oldest daughter, Margaret Ann (Wright) Muller.[100] When Margaret (McCauley) Wright moved, she brought with her the *Wright Family Bible* which she lovingly inscribed and presented to her only living daughter, Margaret Ann (Wright) Muller, shortly before she, herself, passed away on November 4, 1939, at the age of 83.[101] Her obituary appeared in the *Philadelphia Inquirer* on Sunday, November 5, 1939. It read as follows:

> WRIGHT - At Norwood, Pa., Nov. 4, Margaret, widow of Robert Wright, nee
> McCauley formerly of 106 N. Edgewood St., Philadelphia. Funeral services
> Tuesday, 2 P.M., Griffith Chapel, Norwood, Pa. Int. Mount Moriah Cemetery.
> Friends may call Monday evening.[102]

She was buried at Mount Moriah Cemetery alongside her husband, Robert Wright, and her two little boys.

Tom, Loving & Dutiful Son

Thomas "Tom" McCauley did not fare a whole lot better than his sister. When he was 25 years old, he married Mary Ann Wallace, the daughter of Stephen and Letitia (Gormley) Wallace.

Mt. Moriah Cem. Friends may call Mon. eve.

[100]Obituary of Agnes (Wright) Berger, *Philadelphia Inquirer*, Saturday, November 24, 1934, p. 25, Library of Congress, Washington, D.C.

> BERGER - Nov 21, Agnes W., wife of Earl S. Berger, aged 41 years. Services
> Monday, 1:30 P.M. Sechler and McGuire Bldge, 5215 Girard Ave. Interment
> private. Viewing Sunday 7-9 P.M.

[101]*The Wright Family Bible - The New Illuminated Holy Bible ,* (Philadelphia and New York: American Bible House, 1807), in the possession of Kathryn C. Torpey, 5035 Domain Place, Alexandria, Virginia 22311 is inscribed as follows:

> **Presented to**
> *Margaret Muller*
> *From Mother*
> *Virginia Muller Figart*
> *From Margaret Muller*
> *(Mother)*

[102]Obituary of Margaret (McCauley) Wright, *Philadelphia Inquirer*, Sunday, November 5, 1939, p. 9S, Library of Congress, Washington, D.C.

The marriage took place on November 20, 1879, at Tabor Presbyterian Church.[103]

Thomas and Mary Ann (Wallace) McCauley were still living with the Pattons and James McCauley at 1017 Ward Street when their first child, Letitia McCauley, was born on December 6, 1880.[104] The baby was named after Thomas McCauley's mother-in-law, Letitia (Gormley) Wallace, who was also living with them at 1017 Ward Street. Stephen McCauley and his daughter, Margaret McCauley, were probably living there, too, so the house must have been rather crowded.[105]

To alleviate some of the over-crowding in the house, Thomas McCauley moved his family two doors away to 1021 Ward Street in 1882. Tragically, their young daughter, Letitia McCauley, died there on January 1, 1883, from diphtheria of the larynx.[106] Her obituary appeared in the *Philadelphia Public Ledger* on January 2, 1883. It read as follows:

> McCAULEY - On the 1st inst., Letitia, daughter of Thomas and Mary A.
> McCauley, aged 2 years and 3 weeks. The relatives and friends of the family are
> invited at attend the funeral on Wednesday at 1 o'clock from her parents'
> residence No. 1021 Ward Street.[107]

Letitia McCauley was the first of Stephen and Margaret (Wallace) McCauley's grandchildren to die. Ironically, her death and burial coincided almost exactly with the dates of death and burial of her grandmother, Margaret (Wallace) McCauley, 23 years earlier. As was the

---

[103]Marriage Certificate of Thomas McCauley and Mary Ann Wallace, Tabor Presbyterian Church, Philadelphia, Pennsylvania, November 22, 1879, original in the possession of Kathryn C. Torpey, 5035 Domain Place, Alexandria, Virginia 22311. Note: Rev. Robt. Adair, Minister of the Gospel officiated.

[104]Pennsylvania, Philadelphia City Births, 1860-1906, FHL Microfilm Roll 1289320, <<www.familysearch.org>>, downloaded August 24, 2018, re: Letitia McCaully (sic), b. December 6, 1880, Father: Thos. McCaully (sic), Mother: Mary A. McCaully (sic), Book 1880, p. 145.

[105]1880 U.S. Census (population), Pennsylvania, Philadelphia County, City of Philadelphia, Ward 30, E.D. 650, page 109C, lines 44-48, National Archives Microfilm T9, Roll 1189, Household of Nancy Patton & James McCauley.

[106]Pennsylvania, Philadelphia City Death Certificates, 1803-1915, FHL Microfilm Roll 2057400, <<www.familysearch.org>>, downloaded August 24, 2018, re: Letetia (sic) McCaully (sic), d. January 1, 1883, Father: Thomas McCaully (sic), Mother: Mary McCaully (sic), Mount Moriah Cemetery.

[107]Obituary of Letitia McCauley, *Philadelphia Public Ledger*, Tuesday, January 2, 1883, p. 2, Library of Congress, Washington, D.C.

custom, she was buried at Mount Moriah Cemetery.[108]

By 1890, the McCauley family had moved one block north of Ward Street to 1818 Montrose Street and they had three more children - Margaret born October 10, 1883, Letitia (2nd) born July 26, 1885, and Thomas born in October 1888.[109,110,111] Then, tragedy struck again on April 5, 1890, when their young son, Thomas McCauley, died of pneumonia.[112] His obituary appeared in the *Philadelphia Public Ledger* on April 7, 1890. It read as follows:

> McCAULEY - On the 5th inst., Thomas W., son of Thomas and Mary A. McCauley, aged 18 months. The funeral services on Tuesday at 2 o'clock at his parents' residence 1818 Montrose Street, To proceed to Mount Moriah Cemetery.[113]

Two years later, Mary Ann McCauley was born on July 7, 1892.[114] Willis Skillman McCauley, the youngest son of Thomas and Mary Ann (Wallace) McCauley was born on

---

[108]Letter dated December 18, 1985, from Mount Moriah Cemetery, stating that Letitia McCauley was buried in Section 123, Lot 53 on January 4, 1883.

[109]Pennsylvania, Philadelphia City Births, 1860-1906, FHL Microfilm Roll 1289322, <<www.familysearch.org>>, downloaded August 24, 2018, re: Margaret McCaully (sic), b. October 10, 1883, Father: Thomas McCaully (sic), Mother: Mary (sic), Book 1883 p. 376.

[110]Pennsylvania, Philadelphia City Births, 1860-1906, FHL Microfilm Roll 1289324, <<www.familysearch.org>>, downloaded August 24, 2018, re: Letitia McCauley, b. July 26, 1885, Father: Thos. McCauley, Mother: Mary McCauley, Book 1885 p. 254.

[111]Pennsylvania, Philadelphia City Death Certificates, 1803-1915, FHL Microfilm Roll 2080494, <<www.familysearch.org>>, downloaded August 24, 2018, re: Thomas Wallace McCauley, Age at Death: 18 months, d. April 5, 1890, Father: Thos. McCauley, Mother: Mary Ann McCauley, Mount Moriah Cemetery.

[112]Pennsylvania, Philadelphia City Death Certificates, 1803-1915, FHL Microfilm Roll 2080494, <<www.familysearch.org>>, downloaded August 24, 2018, re: Thomas Wallace McCauley, Age at Death: 18 months, d. April 5, 1890, Father: Thos. McCauley, Mother: Mary Ann McCauley, Mount Moriah Cemetery.

[113]Obituary of Thomas W. McCauley, *Philadelphia Public Ledger*, Monday, April 7, 1890, p. 4, Library of Congress, Washington, D.C.

[114]Pennsylvania, Philadelphia City Births, 1860-1906, FHL Microfilm Roll 1289332, <<www.familysearch.org>>, downloaded August 24, 2018, re: Mary McCauley, b. July 7, 1892, Father: Thos. McCauley, Mother: Mary A. (sic), Book 1892 p. 18.

September 8, 1896.[115] He was named after the pastor of Tabor Presbyterian Church. By then, the little house at 1818 Montrose Street was getting rather crowded. In addition to Thomas McCauley and his wife, Mary Ann (Wallace) McCauley, the house was occupied by their four children, Margaret, Letitia (2nd), Mary Ann, and Willis; Thomas McCauley's mother-in-law, Letitia (Gormley) Wallace; and his father, Stephen McCauley.[116]

Apparently, Thomas McCauley's mother-in-law did not entirely approve of her daughter's marriage. According to family legend, Mary Ann (Wallace) McCauley was educated to be a teacher and Thomas McCauley had virtually no education. To disguise his illiteracy, his wife was in the habit of standing behind him and reading out loud over his shoulder. It may have fooled their children, but not his mother-in-law who firmly believed her daughter has married beneath her social class.

Their home was furnished nicely with pieces of furniture provided by Thomas McCauley's mother-in-law. These included a sofa, six parlor chairs, a large chest of drawers, and a marble-topped chest of drawers inscribed with the name of General Winfield Scott Handcock, Company B.   There is no definitive information about where these pieces of furniture came from. The family also had a wooden trunk that belonged to Thomas McCauley's mother-in-law as well as the old battered trunk that Stephen and Margaret (Wallace) McCauley brought with them to America in 1849. With the exception of the living room sofa and the old battered trunk that was falling apart, many of these pieces are still in the family.[117]

Thomas and Mary Ann (Wallace) McCauley also had three framed prints hanging in their living room. One was of Jesus praying; another was of an open Bible with an American flag; and the third was of Betsy Ross, Robert Morris, and George Washington examining the first

---

[115]Letter postmarked July 25, 1995, from Willis Skillman McCauley, Jr., concerning the birth/death dates and places of his parents, Willis Skillman McCauley, Sr., and Mae Schwartz.

[116]1900 U.S. Census (population), Pennsylvania, Philadelphia County, City of Philadelphia, Ward 30, E.D. 0758, page 4, lines 46-50, & page 5, lines 51-53, National Archives Microfilm T623, Roll 1472, Household of Thomas McCauley. Note: These enumeration sheets were mis-transcribed and mis-assembled.

[117]The large chest of drawers, marble-topped chest of drawers, trunk, and two of the parlor chairs are in the possession of Cynthia Scott Chambers, 1450 SW 70th Avenue, Plantation, Florida 33317. Two of the parlor chairs are in the possession of JoAnn Chambers Smith Skinner, 6904 Finian Drive, Wilmington, North Carolina 28409. The remaining two parlor chairs are in the possession of Kathryn C. Torpey, 5035 Domain Place, Alexandria, Virginia 22311.

American flag.[118] The third print was given to their daughter, Margaret McCauley, by the American Flag House and Betsy Ross Association in return for her work raising money for the preservation of the Betsy Ross House located at 239 Arch Street. A large Seth Thomas clock stood on the mantle.[119]

Life appears to have been relatively quiet for the McCauley family until shortly after 1900. On August 2, 1903, after a long life of hard work, Stephen McCauley died of senility at the age of at least 83. His actual date of birth having long since been forgotten and much in dispute, his death certificate reads simply "74 years old."[120] He was buried alongside his wife, Margaret (Wallace) McCauley, at Mount Moriah Cemetery.

At some point, Thomas McCauley had a very bad accident. Family legend has it that he was hit by a train or crushed by a trolley. He lost his left leg. According to his daughter, Mary Ann McCauley, the family received $100.00 in compensation. Thomas McCauley's injuries permanently prevented him from resuming work as a brickmaker. As a result, his three daughters, Margaret, Letitia (2nd), and Mary Ann McCauley, each quit school at 16 to work as a telephone operator for the Bell Telephone Company.

On January 20, 1908, their beloved daughter, Letitia (2nd) McCauley, who was always known as "our Lettie," died at the age of 23 of typhoid fever, the same horrendous disease that killed her grandmother, Margaret (Wallace) McCauley, 48 years earlier.[121] Her obituary appeared in the *Philadelphia Inquirer* on Saturday, February 1, 1908. It read as follows:

> McCauley - On January 30, 1908, Letitia, beloved daughter of Thomas and
> Mary A. McCauley. Relatives and friends, also Philadelphia Council number 10
> D. of L. are invited to attend the funeral on Monday at 2 P.M. from the
> residence of her parents 1818 Montrose Street. Interment at Mount Moriah

---

[118]The Betsy Ross print is in the possession of Kathryn C. Torpey, 5035 Domain Place, Alexandria, Virginia 22311.

[119]The Seth Thomas clock, circa 1885, is in the possession of Cynthia Scott Chambers, 1450 SW 70th Avenue, Plantation, Florida 33317. The label inside it was printed in Waterford, Connecticut.

[120]Pennsylvania, Philadelphia City Death Certificates, 1803-1915, FHL Microfilm Roll 1011832, <<www.familysearch.org>>, downloaded August 24, 2018, re: Stephen McColey (sic) b. 74 years (sic), d. August 2, 1903, Mount Moriah Cemetery.

[121] Pennsylvania Death Certificates,1906-1966, Death Certificate of Lutiera (sic) W. McCauley, b. July 26, 1886 (sic), d. January 30, 1908, Philadelphia, Philadelphia County, Pennsylvania, Father: Thomas, Mother: Mary A. Wallace, <<www.ancestry.com>>, downloaded August 24, 2018.

Cemetery.[122]

Then, on December 31, 1909, the month after their 30th wedding anniversary, Thomas McCauley lost his wife, Mary Ann (Wallace) McCauley, to heart disease.[123] She was only 56 years old. Her obituary appeared in the *Philadelphia Inquirer* on Monday, January 3, 1910. It read as follows:

> McCauley - Entered into rest, Mary A., wife of Thomas McCauley. Relatives
> and friends are invited to attend the funeral on Thursday at 2 P.M., from her late
> residence 1818 Montrose Street. Interment at Mount Moriah Cemetery.[124]

In 1910, the McCauley family was still living at 1818 Montrose Street where Thomas McCauley was enumerated with his three children, Margaret, Mary Ann and Willis McCauley in a home that he owned free and clear of a mortgage.[125] Three years later, in 1912, Thomas McCauley moved his family to West Philadelphia where he bought a house at 1606 S. 53rd Street about 3 blocks away from 1956 S. Ithan Street where the family of his niece, Margaret (Wright) Muller and the Pattons resided.[126,127] Thomas McCauley's mother-in-law, Letitia (Gormley) Wallace (and her furniture) moved with the McCauley family and she resided with them until her

---

[122]Obituary of Letitia McCauley, *Philadelphia Inquirer*, Saturday, February 1, 1908, p. 13, Philadelphia Free Library, Philadelphia, Pennsylvania.

[123]Pennsylvania Death Certificates,1906-1966, Death Certificate of Mary A. McCauley, b. November 25, 1854, d. December 31, 1909, Philadelphia, Philadelphia County, Pennsylvania, Father: Stephen Wallace, Mother: Letitia Gormley, <<www.ancestry.com>>, downloaded August 25, 2018.

[124]Obituary of Mary A. McCauley, *Philadelphia Inquirer*, Monday, January 3, 1910, p. 10, Philadelphia Free Library, Philadelphia, Pennsylvania.

[125]1910 U.S. Census (population), Pennsylvania, Philadelphia County, City of Philadelphia, Ward 30, E.D. 0701, page 2B, lines 91-94, National Archives Microfilm T624 Roll 1400, Household of Thomas McCauley.

[126]1920 U.S. Census (population), Pennsylvania, Philadelphia County, City of Philadelphia, Ward 40, E.D. 1499, page 2B, lines 52-54, National Archives Microfilm T625 Roll 1642, Household of Thos. McCauley. Note: Home owned free of a mortgage.

[127]1920 U.S. Census (population), Pennsylvania, Philadelphia County, City of Philadelphia, Ward 40, E.D. 1498, page 4A, lines 31-34, National Archives Microfilm T625 Roll 1641, Household of August C. Muller. Note: Rented home.

death at the American Oncologic Hospital on October 23, 1914.[128] Her obituary appeared in the *Philadelphia Inquirer* on Saturday, October 24, 1914.[129] As was the custom, she was buried in the McCauley family plot at Mount Moriah Cemetery.

Thomas McCauley spent the rest of his life living at home in West Philadelphia surrounded by his children and their spouses - Mary Ann McCauley who married Henry Grafe Chambers on July 13, 1918; Willis Skillman McCauley who married Mae Schwartz on January 30, 1921, in Elkton, Cecil County, Maryland; and Margaret "Marge" McCauley who married John Smith on October 24, 1925.[130,131,132] He belonged to the Independent Order of Odd Fellows. He helped out around the house whenever he could. He shoveled coal while sitting on an old pine washtub stand in the cellar.[133] And, he cooked dinner for his children whenever they were busy. In fact, he is said to have cooked a spaghetti dinner for everyone the evening his daughter, Mary Ann McCauley, married Henry Grafe Chambers. He had an artificial leg, but by all accounts, preferred to use his crutches as he moved from house to house through the back alleys

---

[128]Pennsylvania Death Certificates,1906-1966, Death Certificate of Letitia Wallace, d. October 23, 1914, American Oncologic Hospital, Philadelphia, Philadelphia County, Pennsylvania, Father: Joseph Gormley, Mother: Margaret Montgomery, <<www.ancestry.com>>, downloaded August 25, 2018.

[129]Obituary of Letitia Wallace, *Philadelphia Inquirer*, Saturday, October 24, 1914, p. 14, and Sunday, October 25, 1914, p. 15, Library of Congress, Washington, D.C.

> Wallace - October 23, 1914, Letitia Wallace, aged 87 years. Relatives and
> friends of the family are invited to attend funeral services Tuesday 2 P.M. from
> the residence of her son-in-law, Thomas McCauley, 1606 S. 53rd Street.
> Interment at Mount Moriah Cemetery.

[130]Marriage Certificate of Henry G. Chambers and Mary Ann McCauley, Philadelphia, Pennsylvania, July 13, 1918, original in the possession of Kathryn C. Torpey, 5035 Domain Place, Alexandria, Virginia 22311. Note: Rev. Freeman D. Bovard, D.D., Methodist Episcopal Minister officiated.

[131]Letter postmarked July 25, 1995, from Willis Skillman McCauley, Jr., concerning the marriage of his parents, Willis Skillman McCauley, Sr., and Mae Schwartz, on January 30, 1921, in Elkton, Cecil County, Maryland.

[132]Marriage Record of John Smith and Margaret McCauley dated October 24, 1925, Tabor Presbyterian Church, Presbyterian Church Records, 1874-1940, Presbyterian Historical Society, Philadelphia, Pennsylvania, <<www.ancestry.com>>, downloaded June 28, 2018.

[133]The old pine washtub stand was in the possession of Cynthia Scott Chambers, 1450 SW 70th Avenue, Plantation, Florida 33317 until 1992 when it finally succumbed to dry rot.

of his neighborhood in West Philadelphia.[134] He lived long enough to know all three of his grandsons, William Scott Chambers, Thomas Wallace Chambers and Willis Skillman McCauley, Jr. He died on August 8, 1925, at the age of 71 and was buried in Mount Moriah Cemetery.[135] His obituary appeared in the *Philadelphia Public Ledger* on Tuesday, August 11, 1925. It read as follows:

> McCAULEY - Entered into rest, Aug. 8, THOMAS, husband of the late Mary A. McCauley. Relatives and friends, also United Lodge, No. 719, I.O.O.F., invited to attend funeral, Wed., 2 P.M., residence, 1606 S. 53^d st. Int. Mt. Moriah Cem. Friends may call Tues. eve.[136]

WHEN AT LAST THE DAWN BROKE

Next year, September 7, 2019, will mark the 170th anniversary of the arrival of Stephen and Margaret (Wallace) McCauley in America. We can only surmise that when at last the dawn broke on their final day at sea and for the first time they saw the faint outline of the coast of New York, they must have been truly thankful to God for having spared them long enough to complete that part of their journey. Despite hardships and sorrow as they forged their new life in America, they never once looked back. Their legacy, the result of their courage in risking it all for a better life in America, is us, their combined 50 plus descendants. For this singular act of selflessness in seeking a better life in America for their family, we, their descendants, will be forever grateful.

-----

[134]Principally, the home he shared with his daughter, Margaret McCauley, at 1606 S. 53rd Street; the home of his daughter, Mary Ann (McCauley) Chambers at 1514 S. Lindenwood Street; the home of his son, Willis Skillman McCauley, Sr., at 1503 S. Lindenwood Street, and the home of his niece, Margaret (Wright) Muller at 1956 S. Ithan Street which was also occupied by his first cousin, William Patton, and his wife, Ella (Stewart) Patton.

[135]Pennsylvania Death Certificates,1906-1966, Death Certificate of Thomas McCauley, b. February 14, 1854, d. August 8, 1925, Philadelphia, Philadelphia County, Pennsylvania, Father: Stephen, Mother: Margaret Wallace, <<www.ancestry.com>>, downloaded August 25, 2018.

[136]Obituary of Thomas McCauley, *Philadelphia Public Ledger*, Tuesday, August 11, 1925, p. 18, Library of Congress, Washington, D.C.

Certificate of Marriage
Aghadowey Presbyterian Church
County Londonderry, Ireland
Stephen McAuley & Margaret Wallace
July 11, 1848

1848 Marriage solemnized at Aghadowey
11th July   Stephen McAuley - Bachelor Mullahinch
    Margret Wallace Spinster   Do
Married in the Presbyterian church Aghadowey
according to the form of the Presbyterian church
in Ireland by me John Brown
This marriage   { Stephen McAuley
was solemnized   { Margret Wallace
between us   { Robert Wallace
        In presence of us { William Lyons

Extracted from the marriage register Aghadowey

        John Brown P. M.
    Wm Heancy Session Clerk

Extract of the Marriage Register, Aghadowey Presbyterian Church, County Londonderry, Ireland, July 11, 1848, original in the possession of Kathryn C. Torpey, 5035 Domain Place, Alexandria, Virginia 22311.

Marriage Certificate of Thomas McCauley and Mary Ann Wallace, Tabor Presbyterian Church, Philadelphia, Pennsylvania, November 22, 1879, original in the possession of Kathryn C. Torpey, 5035 Domain Place, Alexandria, Virginia 22311.

Marriage Certificate of Henry Grafe Chambers and Mary A. McCauley, Philadelphia, Pennsylvania, July 30, 1918, original in the possession of Kathryn C. Torpey, 5035 Domain Place, Alexandria, Virginia 22311.

Appendix C

Certificate of Marriage
Tabor Presbyterian Church
John Smith & Margaret McCauley
Philadelphia, Pennsylvania
October 24, 1925

Marriage Certificate of John Smith and Margaret McCauley, Tabor Presbyterian Church, Philadelphia, Pennsylvania, October 24, 1925, original in the possession of Kathryn C. Torpey, 5035 Domain Place, Alexandria, Virginia 22311.

Appendix D

THE NEW ILLUMINATED

HOLY BIBLE

SELF-PRONOUNCING

WITH MARGINAL REFERENCES AND CONCORDANCE

800 ORIGINAL ILLUSTRATIONS

CONTAINING THE OLD AND NEW TESTAMENTS: TRANSLATED
OUT OF THE ORIGINAL TONGUES: AND WITH THE
FORMER TRANSLATIONS DILIGENTLY
COMPARED AND REVISED

*(THE TEXT CONFORMS TO THAT OF THE OXFORD BIBLE
PRINTED AT THE UNIVERSITY PRESS, OXFORD)*

AMERICAN BIBLE HOUSE
PHILADELPHIA and NEW YORK

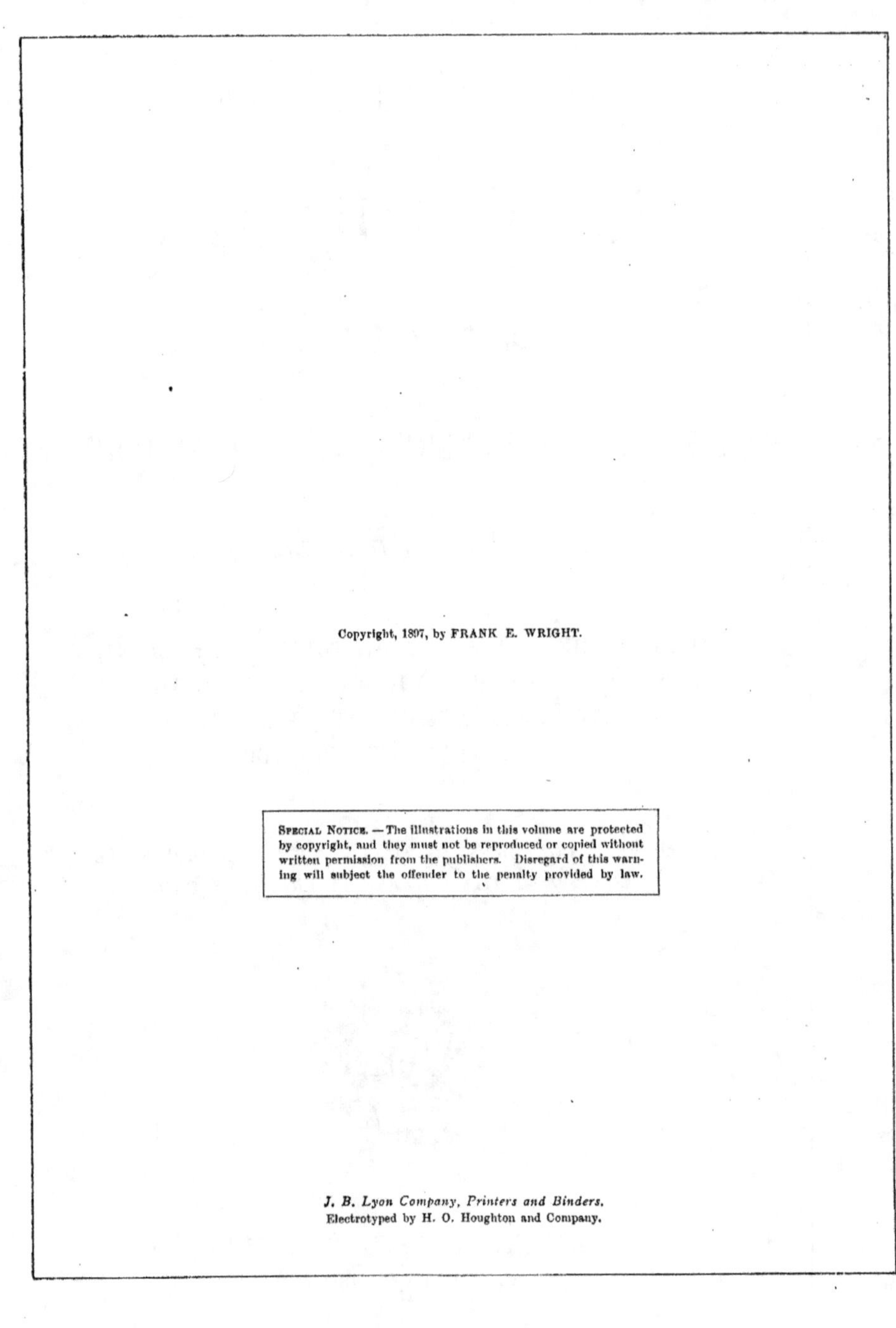

Copyright, 1897, by FRANK E. WRIGHT.

J. B. Lyon Company, Printers and Binders.
Electrotyped by H. O. Houghton and Company.

I AM THE WORD
Presented to
Margaret Muller
From Mother

Virginia Muller Figart
From Margaret Muller
(Mother)

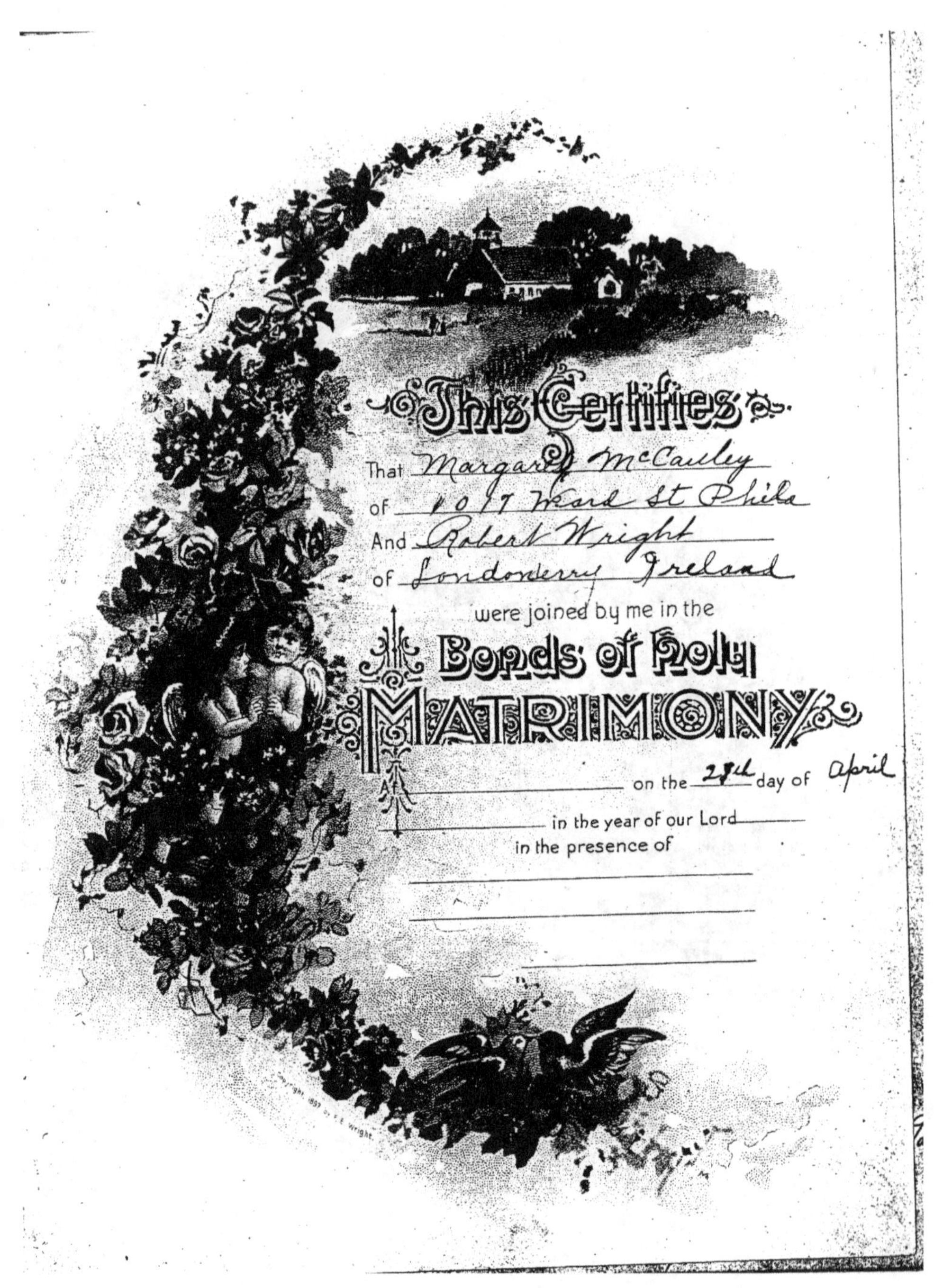
This Certifies
That Margaret J. McCauley
of 1017 Ward St Phila
And Robert Wright
of Londonderry Ireland
were joined by me in the
Bonds of Holy
MATRIMONY
on the 28th day of April
in the year of our Lord
in the presence of

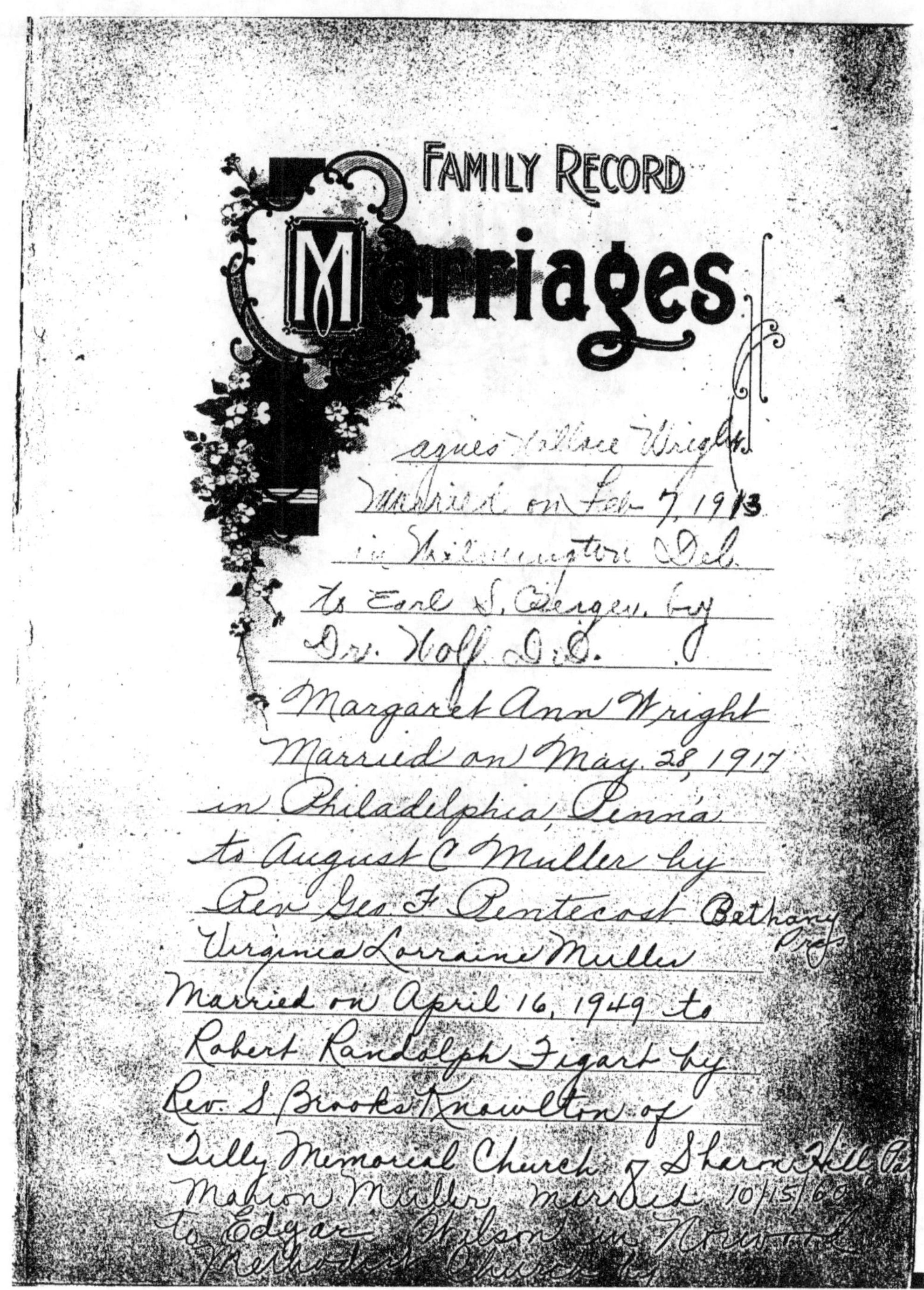

Agnes Wallace Wright
Married on Feb 7, 1913
in Wilmington Del.
to Earl S. Berger, by
Dr. Wolf, D.D.

Margaret Ann Wright
Married on May 28, 1917
in Philadelphia, Penna.
to August C Muller by
Rev Geo F Pentecost Bethany Pres.

Virginia Lorraine Muller
Married on April 16, 1949 to
Robert Randolph Figart by
Rev. S Brooks Knowlton of
Tully Memorial Church, Sharon Hill Pa

Marion Muller married 10/15/60
to Edgar Wilson in New
Methodist Church

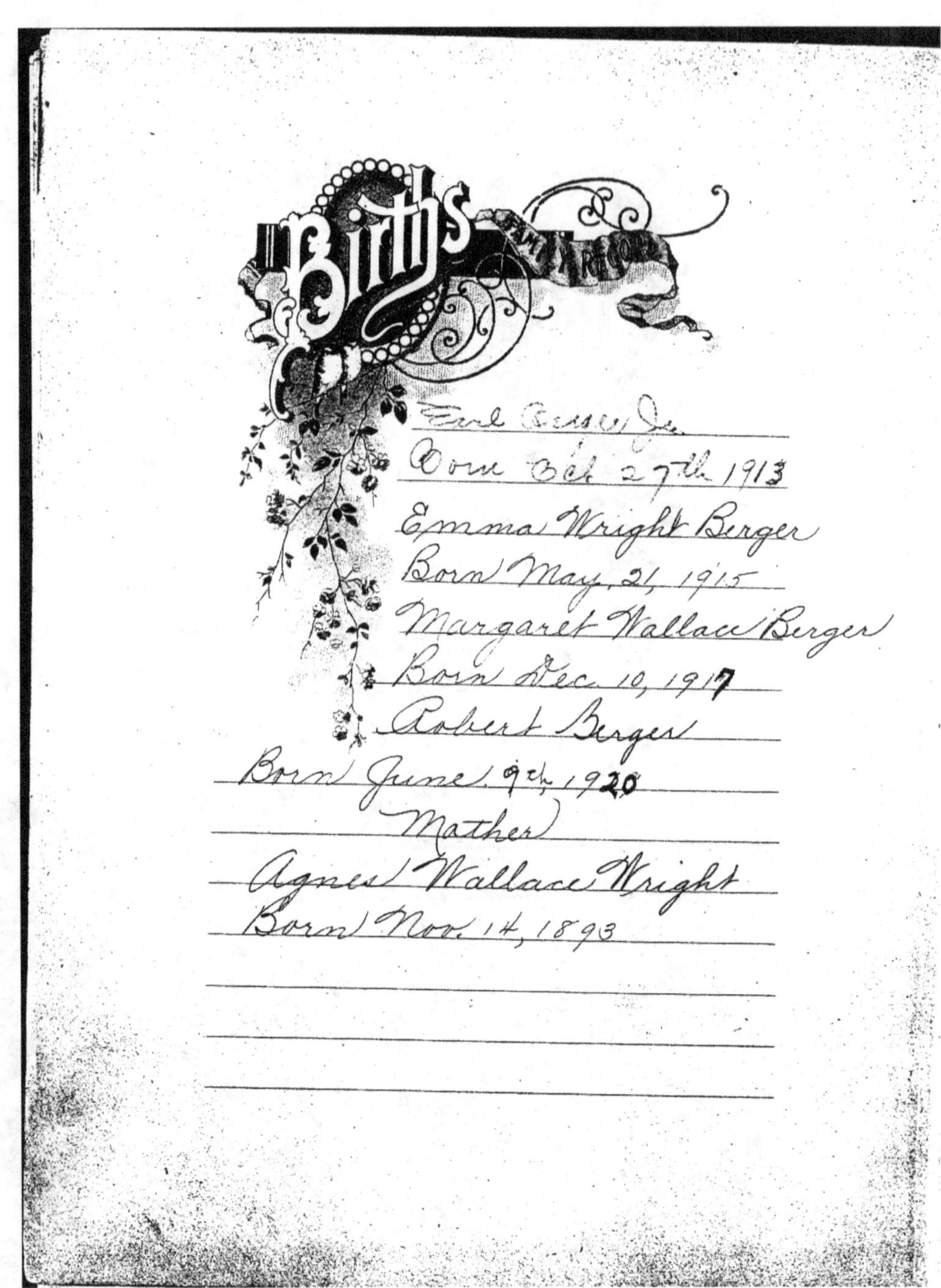

Births
Family Record

Earl Berger Jr.
Born Feb 27th 1913
Emma Wright Berger
Born May, 21, 1915
Margaret Wallace Berger
Born Dec. 10, 1917
Robert Berger
Born June 9th, 1920
Mother
Agnes Wallace Wright
Born Nov. 14, 1893

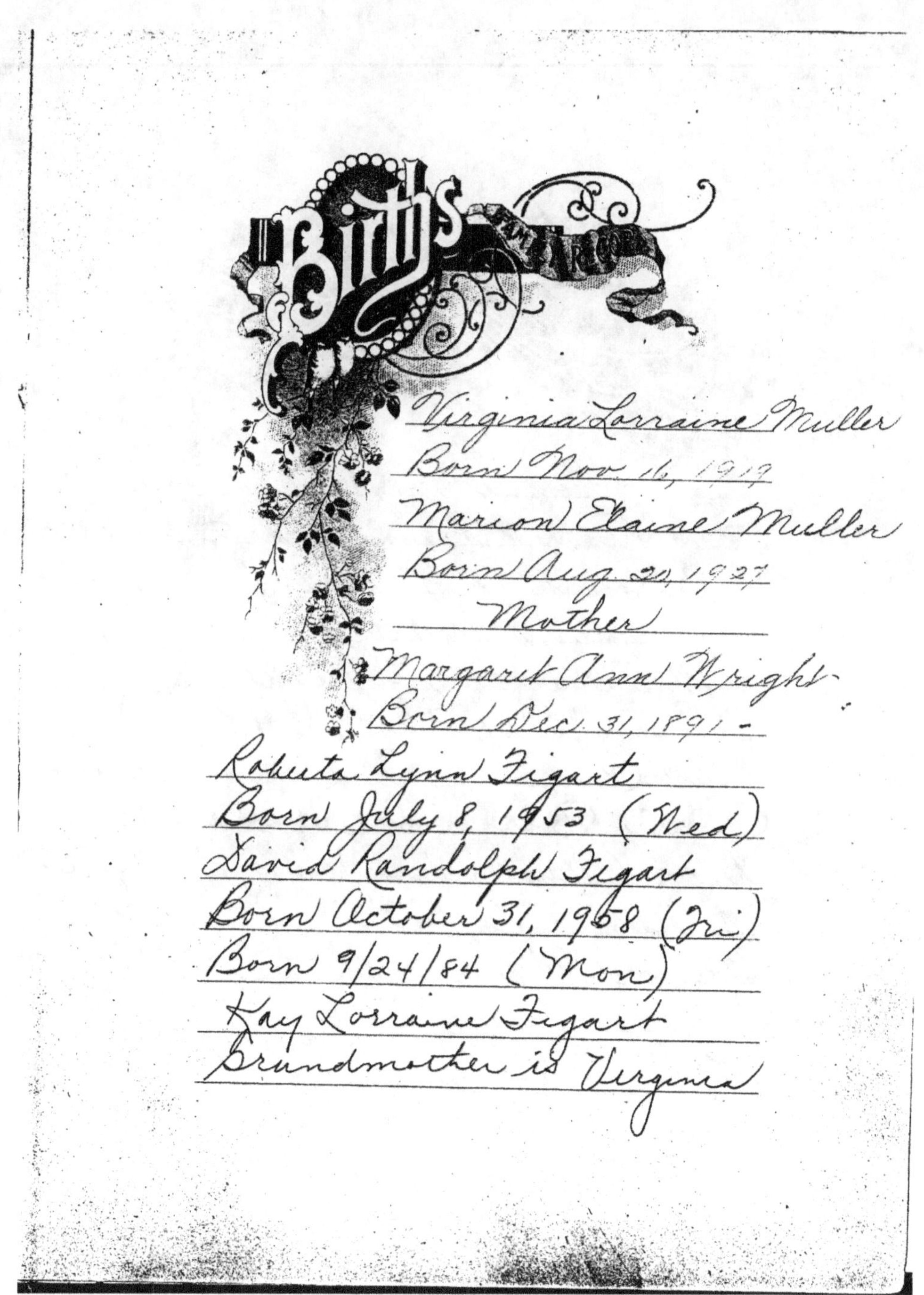

Virginia Lorraine Muller
Born Nov 16, 1919
Marion Elaine Muller
Born Aug 20, 1927
Mother
Margaret Ann Wright
Born Dec. 31, 1891 -
Roberta Lynn Figart
Born July 8 1953 (Wed)
David Randolph Figart
Born October 31, 1958 (Fri)
Born 9/24/84 (Mon)
Kay Lorraine Figart
Grandmother is Virginia

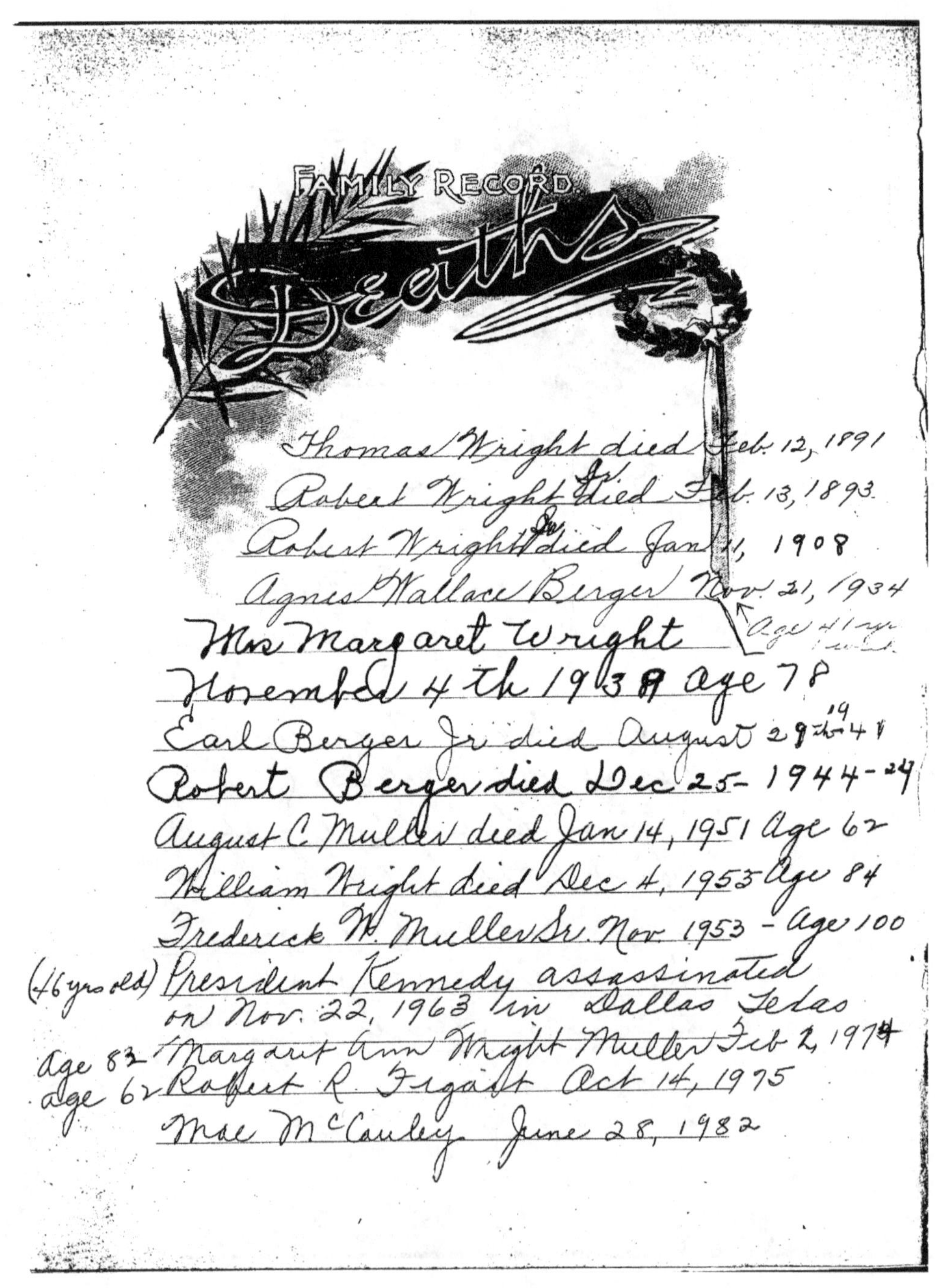

FAMILY RECORD
Deaths

Thomas Wright died Feb. 12, 1891
Robert Wright Sr died Feb. 13, 1893.
Robert Wright Jr died Jan 11, 1908
Agnes Wallace Berger Nov. 21, 1934
Age 41 yr
Mrs Margaret Wright
November 4th 1938 Age 78
Earl Berger Jr died August 29th 1948
Robert Berger died Dec 25 - 1944 - 24
August C Muller died Jan 14, 1951 Age 62
William Wright died Dec 4, 1953 Age 84
Frederick W. Muller Sr. Nov 1953 - Age 100
(46 yrs old) President Kennedy assassinated
on Nov. 22, 1963 in Dallas Texas
Age 83 Margaret Ann Wright Muller Feb 2, 1974
Age 62 Robert R Figart Oct 14, 1975
Mae McCauley June 28, 1982

Margaret (McCauley) Smith
1883-1957

Margaret (McCauley) Smith was the oldest surviving daughter of Thomas and Mary Ann (Wallace) McCauley. She was born October 19, 1883 in Philadelphia and baptized on April 13, 1884 at Tabor Presbyterian Church. She left school at age 16 to work as a telephone operator for the Bell Telephone Company of Pennsylvania from where she retired on November 1, 1921.

She lived with her widowed father at 1606 S. 53rd Street in West Philadelphia. He had lost his left leg when he was hit by a train or crushed by a trolley. The injury had permanently prevented him from resuming work as a brickmaker.

Margaret (McCauley) Smith was a member of Tabor Presbyterian Church. She was also very patriotic. The American Flag House and Betsy Ross Memorial Association presented her with the following print known as "Birth of our nation's flag," dated June 14, 1898 for her fund raising support to save the Betsy Ross House in Philadelphia. The print shows an interior scene with General George Washington seated on the left with Robert Morris, and standing, the Honorable George Ross, and with Betsy Ross seated on the right holding "our Nation's Flag."

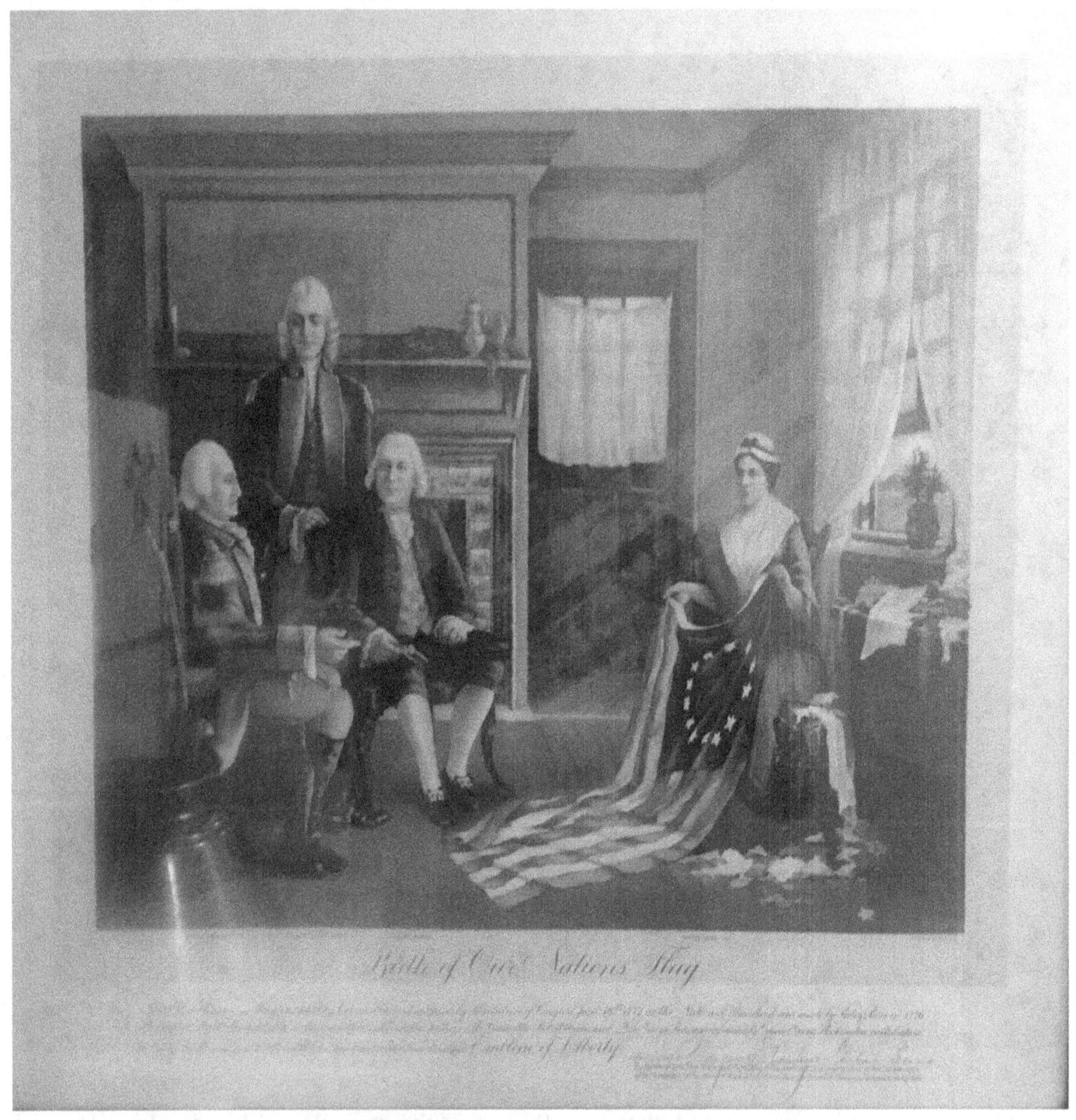

Presented to Margaret McCauley of Phila, Penna.
by the American Flag House and Betsy Ross Memorial Association for aiding in the preservation
of the Birthplace of Our Nation's Flag and for the erection of a National Memorial in honor of Betsy Ross.

She married John Smith on October 24, 1925, at Tabor Presbyterian Church about 3 months after the death of her father. According to family legend, her hesitancy in marrying John Smith was the fact that he had been previously married and the marriage was dissolved by divorce. Her father is said to have encouraged her to marry John Smith regardless of the divorce because he was a "good man." Fortunately, she took her father's advice.

This Certifies

That _John Smith_
of _Philadelphia, Penna_
and _Margaret McCauley_
of _Philadelphia, Penna_

were by me united in the bonds of

Marriage

at _the Tabor Presbyterian Manse_
on the _24th_ day of _October_
in the year of our Lord Nineteen Hundred and
Twenty five

conformably to the ordinance of God and the Laws of the State.

Abram M. Long
MINISTER OF THE GOSPEL

WITNESSES PRESENT AT THE MARRIAGE

The marriage ceremony was followed by a gathering of family and friends. Those who signed the guest book included Margaret (McCauley) Smith's sister, Mary Ann (McCauley) Chambers & Harry G. Chambers; her brother, Willis S. McCauley & Mae (Schwartz) McCauley; her cousin, Margaret A. (Wright) Muller; her husband's brother, Willard A. Smith; his sisters, Ethel (Smith) Griest, Roberta C. (Smith) Griest, Mary (Smith) Bannister, & Clara (Smith) Liddle; his nephew, Jessye Liddle; and his best friend, Robert Allen Hall, among others.

CONGRATULATIONS

A. W. Song
A. Eleanor Song
Mary McC. Chambers
Margaret A. McCider
Willis S. McCauley
Mae S. Mc M. Cauley
Harry G. Chambers
Willard A. Smith
Ethel S. Griest
Roberta C. Griest

CONGRATULATIONS

Mr. & Mrs. Thos. Reif
Mary J. Kelly
Mary H. Fleming
Mrs. Mabel M. Crehen
Mrs. James G. Coles
Lillie A. Roberts
Mary C. McGoshan
S. Mary Kindberg
Mae W. Armstrong
Jessye S. Liddell
Clara H. Liddell

CONGRATULATIONS

Alexander Elliott
John F. Reif
Florence M. Reif
Elmer B. Reif
Mr. & Mrs. Philip Reif
Elizabeth Elliott
George C. Stevenson
Margaret T. Stevenson
Scott A. Hall

CONGRATULATIONS

Anna E. Rockey
Margaret W. Meyer
Tillie Proctor
Leah J. Wilson
Mary L. Wilson
Martha Gordon
Harry F. W. Meyer
Mary Bannister

The couple may have met as early as 1920 while Uncle John was living at 1625 S. 53rd Street which was in the same block as the McCauley residence. Reportedly, they had a good life together. Margaret (McCauley) Smith had no children of her own, but her nephews - Bill Chambers, Tom Chambers, and Skill McCauley - were very fond of her.

They called her Aunt Marge. Her nephew, Bill Chambers, remembered her as amusing and nice. In fact, he said she was quite funny at times, though often unintentionally. In fact, all three of Aunt Marge's nephews saw her quite often because they lived only a block away from her in homes located at opposite ends of Lindenwood Street. The Chambers family owned their home at 1547 S. Lindenwood Street and the McCauley family had a mortgage on their home at 1503 S. Lindenwood Street. All three of her nephews were baptized at Tabor Presbyterian Church. And, they attended Bible school at that church under the watchful eye of Aunt Marge.

According to her nephew, Bill Chambers, Aunt Marge bought out the shares of her sister, Mary Ann (McCauley) Chambers, and her brother, Uncle Willis McCauley, to the house at 1606 S. 53rd Street after the death of their father in 1925. When Aunt Marge died in 1957, she left the house to her widowed sister, Mary Ann (McCauley) Chambers. The house was originally forced air and coal. It was converted to radiators and coal (hot water), and later to gas.

Uncle John was an insurance agent who also owned some rental houses in Philadelphia. His best friend, Allen Hall, was also an insurance agent. As insurance agents, they both made frequent home visits to their clients to collect insurance premiums. Uncle John also made frequent visits to his tenants to collect rent payments. In fact, Uncle Willis McCauley is said to have driven Uncle John around in his Model A Ford when Uncle John went to collect the insurance premiums and the rent. Apparently, Uncle John did quite well in business because he and Aunt Marge had enough money in their savings accounts that they were able to pay off the house at 1606 S. 53rd Street and help Uncle Willis to pay off the house at 1503 S. Lindenwood

Street when he could no longer make the mortgage payments during the Great Depression. As a
result, neither family lost their home to foreclosure.

Uncle John and Aunt Marge also owned stock. Surviving, presumably worthless, stock
certificates include 10 shares of capital stock in Manufacturers' Title and Trust Company; 1 share
of common stock and 2 shares of preferred stock in Granitepier Finance Company; and 150
shares of capital stock in Insurance Finance Corporation. All but 1 of these stock certificates
were issued before the stock market crashed on October 29, 1929.

Aunt Marge's nephew, Bill Chambers also recalled that after his father, Henry G.
Chambers, bought a 1936 Plymouth, they used the car to visit their Muller cousins who had
moved from 1956 W. Ithan Street in West Philadelphia to 38 W. Winona Avenue in Norwood,
Delaware County, Pennsylvania. They also used the car for occasional trips to Liberty Grove in
Cecil County, Maryland, to visit Uncle John's family, presumably his sisters, Ethel (Smith)
Griest and Roberta C. (Smith) Griest, and possibly his sister, Mary (Smith) Bannister, one of
whom is said to have made the beautiful quilt that is still in the family today.

Sometime during the Great Depression, Uncle John's daughter from his first marriage
came to visit. She stayed with Uncle John and Aunt Marge for a few days. Reportedly, everyone
was shocked to find out that Uncle John had a daughter by a previous marriage.

Uncle John died on February 24, 1949. Aunt Marge died on May 1, 1957. Their
obituaries appeared in the *Philadelphia Inquirer* on Saturday, February 26, 1949, and Saturday,
May 4, 1957, respectively.

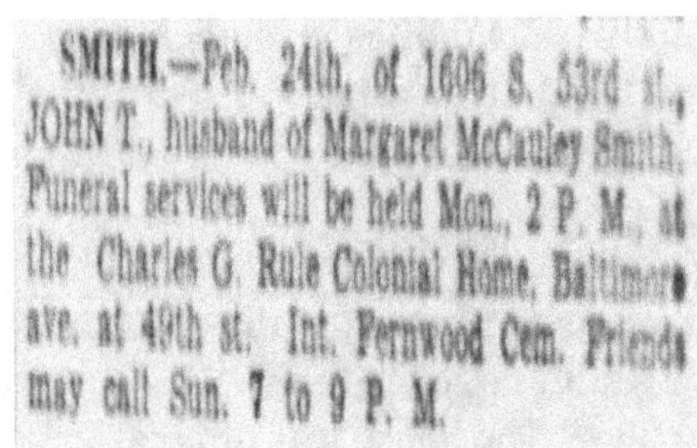

SMITH.—Feb. 24th, of 1606 S. 53rd st.,
JOHN T., husband of Margaret McCauley Smith.
Funeral services will be held Mon., 2 P. M., at
the Charles G. Rule Colonial Home, Baltimore
ave. at 49th st. Int. Fernwood Cem. Friends
may call Sun. 7 to 9 P. M.

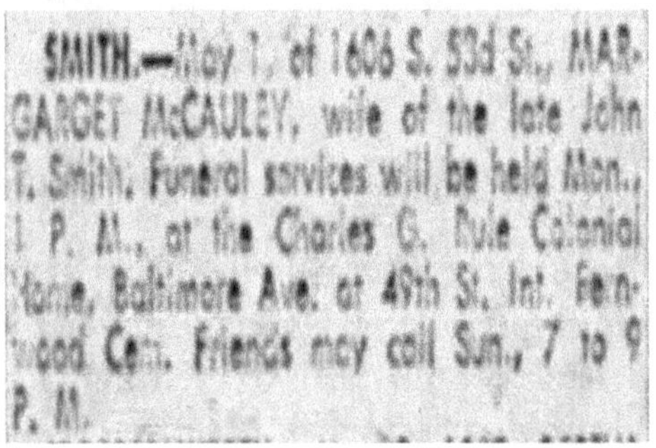

SMITH.—May 1, of 1606 S. 53d St., MAR-
GARET McCAULEY, wife of the late John
T. Smith. Funeral services will be held Mon.,
1 P. M., at the Charles G. Rule Colonial
Home, Baltimore Ave. at 49th St. Int. Fern-
wood Cem. Friends may call Sun., 7 to 9
P. M.

They are both buried in Fernwood Cemetery in Lot Number 307 of Section 50 in the
same plot as Uncle John's young son, James Allen Smith, who died on April 10, 1911, at the age
of 5 when he was hit by a trolley in front of his house when he ran outside to play.

Extensive research was conducted to identify the name of the first wife and daughter of
Uncle John Smith. The following Memorandum for the Record was prepared to document the
results of that research. Unfortunately, there are no living descendants of Uncle John's first wife
and daughter.

MEMORANDUM FOR THE RECORD   MCCAULEY FILE: 167McC

BY: Kathryn C. Torpey
       5035 Domain Place
       Alexandria VA 22311

DATE: 7 July 2018

FOCUS: The first wife and daughter of John Thomas Smith (1872-1949), husband of Margaret McCauley.

BACKGROUND: According to family legend, John Thomas Smith was an insurance salesman who owned some houses in Philadelphia that he rented out. His best friend was Allen Hall also an insurance agent. John Thomas Smith was married twice. Nothing was known about his first wife and their family except that they had a son (name unknown) who was said to have died at about the age of 5. They were also said to have had a daughter (name unknown) who visited with John Thomas Smith and his second wife, Margaret McCauley, for a few days in the 1930s. Reportedly, everyone was shocked to find out that John Thomas Smith had a daughter by a previous marriage.[1]

METHODOLOGY: Based on the above-described family conversation that took place in 1996 and an old cemetery deed in the possession of the family, it was possible to identify the burial location of John Thomas Smith and his second wife, Margaret (McCauley) Smith, as well as his son from his first marriage named James Allen Smith.[2] Almost all of the subsequent research to determine the identity of the first wife and daughter of John Thomas Smith took place in 2018 as preparations began for correlating and compiling evidence in support of writing the McCauley family history. Most of the research was undertaken using on-line resources with the exception of vital records requested from the Pennsylvania State Archives, the New Jersey State Archives, and the Illinois Department of Vital Records.

RESEARCH RESULTS: Research revealed the following evidence:

----

[1]Conversation on 21 July 1996, with the late William Scott Chambers, 325 N.W. 95th Avenue, Plantation, FL 33324-7021.

[2]Deed No. 13246, dated 10 May (sic) 1911 from The Fernwood Company to John T. Smith for Lot 307, Section 50 at Fernwood Cemetery, Book 1, p. 615, in the possession of Kathryn C. Torpey, McCauley File: 48McC, states:

> James A. Smith interred April 15, 1911
> John T. Smith interred Feb. 28, 1949
> Margaret McC Smith interred May 6, 1957

1.   MARRIAGE RECORDS

a.   On 27 August 1903, John T. Smith and Lillian Killeen were married at
Abigail Vare Methodist Episcopal Church in Philadelphia, Pennsylvania.[3]
Their marriage license application dated 1 August 1903 states that he was
a "collector" born in Maryland on 3 March 1875 (sic) and she was a
"stenographer" born in Pennsylvania on 22 February 1882. Neither was
previously married. The marriage return confirms that the couple was
married on 27 August 1903.[4]

b.   On 17 August 1914, Lillian Killeen and William M. Rowe were married in
Camden, New Jersey, by the Rev. Charles Bowden. She is stated to have
been born in Philadelphia, aged 32 years, the daughter of John Killeen and
Anna McPherson, and he is stated to be a "compositor," born in
Philadelphia, aged 26 years, the son of William R. Rowe and Lillian Fair.
According to the marriage record, she was once previously married.[5]

c.   On 24 October 1925, John Smith and Margaret McCauley were married at
Tabor Presbyterian Church in Philadelphia, Pennsylvania.[6] Their marriage
license application dated 22 October 1925 states that John Smith was an
"agent" born in Maryland on 3 March 1872 (sic). It further states that he
was once previously married and that the marriage was terminated by
divorce on 19 January 1914. The marriage return confirms that the couple
was married on 24 October 1925.[7]

---

[3]Marriage Record of John T. Smith and Lillian Killeen dated 27 August 1903, Abigail
Vare Methodist Episcopal Church, Historic Pennsylvania Church and Town Records, Historical
Society of Pennsylvania, Philadelphia, Pennsylvania, <<www.ancestry.com>>, downloaded 4
June 2018.

[4]Affidavit of Applicant for Marriage License [with Return], # 164419, 1 August 1903,
(John T. Smith & Lillian Killeen), Philadelphia, Pennsylvania Civil Marriages, 1677-1950,
<<www.familysearch.org>>, downloaded 28 May 2018.

[5]Certificate and Record of Marriage of William M. Rowe and Lillian Killeen dated 17
August 1914, New Jersey State Archives, P.O. Box 307, Trenton, NJ 08625-0307.

[6]Marriage Record of John Smith and Margaret McCauley dated 24 October 1925, Tabor
Presbyterian Church, Presbyterian Church Records, 1874-1940, Presbyterian Historical Society,
Philadelphia, Pennsylvania, <<www.ancestry.com>>, downloaded 28 June 2018.

[7]Affidavit of Applicant for Marriage License [with Return], # 520445, 22 October 1925,
(John Smith & Margaret McCauley), Philadelphia, Pennsylvania Civil Marriages, 1677-1950,

2.   BIRTH RECORDS

    a.   On 14 January 1906, James Allen Smith was born in Philadelphia, Pennsylvania to John T. Smith and Lillian Killen (sic).[8]

    b.   On 27 May 1912, Dorothy Allen Smith was born in Philadelphia, Pennsylvania to John T. Smith and Lily Killen (sic).[9]

3.   BAPTISMAL RECORDS

    a.   On 23 December 1906, James Allen Smith was baptized at All Saints Episcopal Church in Philadelphia, Pennsylvania. His birth date is listed as 14 January 1906. His parents were stated to be John Thomas Smith and Lillian Smith.[10]

    b.   On 5 June 1915, Dorothy Allan (sic) Rowe, was baptized at Saint James the Less Episcopal Church in Philadelphia, Pennsylvania. Her birth date is listed as 27 May 1912. Her parents were stated to be William Matthew Rowe and Lillian Rowe.[11]

4.   DEATH RECORDS

    a.   On 10 April 1911, James A. Smith died as a result of an accident in Philadelphia, Pennsylvania. His birth date is listed as 17 (sic) January 1906 and his parents were listed as John T. Smith and Lillian Killeen. He

---

<<www.familysearch.org>>, downloaded 28 June 2018.

[8]Birth Certificate of James Allen Smith, 14 January 1906, Philadelphia, Pennsylvania, Pennsylvania, Birth Certificates, 1906-1910, <<www.ancestry.com>>, downloaded 30 June 2018.

[9]Birth Certificate of Dorothy Allen Smith, 27 May 1912, Philadelphia, Pennsylvania, Pennsylvania State Archives, Harrisburg, Pennsylvania 17120-0090.

[10]Baptism of John Allen Smith, 23 December 1906, All Saints Episcopal Church, Philadelphia, Pennsylvania, Pennsylvania and New Jersey Church and Town Records, 1669-2013, <<www.ancestry.com>>, downloaded 1 July 2018.

[11]Baptism of Dorothy Allan (sic) Rowe, 5 June 1915, Saint James the Less Episcopal Church, Philadelphia, Pennsylvania, Pennsylvania and New Jersey Church and Town Records, 1669-2013, <<www.ancestry.com>>, downloaded 30 May 2018.

was buried at Fernwood Cemetery in Delaware County, Pennsylvania.[12]

b.   On 24 February 1949, John Thomas Smith died as a result of pneumonia in Philadelphia, Pennsylvania. His birth date is listed as 3 March 1872. He was buried at Fernwood Cemetery in Delaware County, Pennsylvania.[13]

c.   On 1 May 1957, Margaret (McCauley) Smith died as result of a cerebral hemorrhage in Philadelphia, Pennsylvania. Her birth date is listed as 10 October 1883. She was buried at Fernwood Cemetery in Delaware County, Pennsylvania.[14]

d.   On 24 September 1968, Lillian Rowe died as a result of acute cardiac digitation in Cook County, Illinois. Her death date is listed as 24 September 1968. Her birth date and place are listed as 22 February 1882 in Pennsylvania and her parents were listed as John Killeen and Annie McPherson. The informant is identified as Dorothy Kinniburgh, daughter. She was buried in Chapel Hill Gardens West in DuPage County, Illinois.[15]

5.   HEADSTONE RECORDS

a.   The Smith family headstone at Fernwood Cemetery, Delaware County, Pennsylvania, reads:

SMITH
1872 JOHN THOMAS 1949
1883 MARGARET McC 1957
1906 JAMES ALLAN (sic) 1911[16]

---

[12]Death Certificate of James A. Smith, 10 April 1911, Philadelphia, Pennsylvania, Pennsylvania Death Certificates, 1906-1966, <<www.ancestry.com>>, downloaded 1 July 2018.

[13]Death Certificate of John Thomas Smith, 24 February 1949, Philadelphia, Pennsylvania, Pennsylvania Death Certificates, 1906-1966, <<www.ancestry.com>>, downloaded 1 July 2018.

[14]Death Certificate of Margaret (McCauley) Smith, 1 May 1957, Philadelphia, Pennsylvania, Pennsylvania Death Certificates, 1906-1966, <<www.ancestry.com>>, downloaded 30 June 2018.

[15]Death Certificate of Lillian Rowe, 24 September 1968, Cook County, Illinois, Illinois Department of Public Health, Springfield, Illinois 62702-2737.

[16]Find-A-Grave Memorial # 145031788, John Thomas Smith (headstone photograph), added 15 April 2015, Fernwood Cemetery, Delaware County, Pennsylvania,

b.   The Lillian Rowe headstone at Chapel Hill Gardens West, DuPage
      County, Illinois, reads:

> LILLIAN ROWE
> FEB. 22, 1882
> SEPT. 24, 1968[17]

c.   The Kinniburgh family headstone at Chapel Hill Gardens West, DuPage
      County, Illinois, reads:

> JAMES A.   DOROTHY A.
> 1916-2001   1912-2004
>   KINNIBURGH[18]

6.   OBITUARIES

a.   Obituary of Lillian Rowe, dated 25 September 1968.[19]

> Lillian Rowe, nee Killeen, of Broadview,
> beloved wife of the late William M. Sr.;
> loving mother of Dorothy (James) Kin-
> niburgh, and William M. Jr., (Betty);
> grandmother of Thomas and Susan. Visi-
> tation after 7 p.m., Wednesday, at
> Broadview Funeral Home, 2020 Roosevelt
> road, Broadview. Services Thursday, Sept.
> 26, 11 a.m., at chapel. Interment
> Chapel Hill Gardens West. Please omit
> flowers.

<<www.findagrave.com>>, downloaded 1 July 2018.

[17]Find-A-Grave Memorial # 150042516, Lillian Rowe (headstone photograph), added 31
July 2015, Chapel Hill Gardens West, DuPage County, Illinois, <<www.findagrave.com>>,
downloaded 1 July 2018.

[18]Find-A-Grave Memorial # 129582954, Dorothy A. Kinniburgh (headstone photograph),
added 10 May 2014, Chapel Hill Gardens West, DuPage County, Illinois,
<<www.findagrave.com>>, downloaded 1 July 2018.

[19]Obituary of Lillian Rowe, 25 September 1968, Wednesday, *Chicago Tribune*, Chicago,
Illinois, <<www.newspapers.com>>, downloaded 30 May 2018.

b.	Obituary of Dorothy A. Kinniburgh, dated 4 April 2004.[20]

> Dorothy A. Kinniburgh, age 91, longtime resi-
> dent of Broadview, passed away Thursday at
> her home. Beloved wife of the late James; lov-
> ing sister of William M. (the late Betty J.) Rowe;
> dear aunt of Thomas (Gloria) Rowe and Susan
> (Dieter) Fleischhauer. Dorothy was a Sunday
> School Teacher at Immanuel Lutheran Church
> in Broadview where she was a very active
> member of the Womens Auxiliary and Church
> Council. Visitation Monday 12 noon until time
> of service at 2 p.m. at Chapel Hills Gardens
> West Funeral Home, 17W201 Roosevelt Rd.,
> (1 blk W. of Rt. 83), Oak Brook Terrace. Inter-
> ment Chapel Hill Gardens West Cemetery. For
> info 630-941-5860
> Sign Guestbook at chicagotribune.com/obituaries

c.	Obituary of William M. Rowe, Jr., dated 10 May 2012.[21]

> William M. Rowe, WWII and Korean War, USAF B29
> Pilot, age 88, beloved husband of the late Betty Jane,
> nee Lindstrom (2000). Loving father of Thomas T.
> Rowe and Susan Lynn (Dieter) Fleischhauer. Cherished
> grandfather of Brittany A. Rowe, Joshua (Kimberly)
> Fleishhauer, and Karen (Scott) Jones. Dearest great-
> grandfather of Emily and Kara. Fond brother of the late
> Dorothy Kinniburg (sic). Dear friend of Ethel Korycki.
> Visitation Friday, January 20, 2012 from 3-9 PM.
> Funeral Services Saturday, January 21, 2012 at 11:00 a.m.
> at Colonial Chapel 15525 S. 73rd Ave (155th/Wheeler Dr.
> & Harlem) Orland Park, IL. Interment private at Chapel
> Hill Gardens West Cemetery. Express your thoughts and
> condolences at www.colonialchapel.com 708-532-5400.

7.	SOCIAL SECURITY CLAIMS INDEX (SSCI)

a.	Lillian Killeen Rowe, born: 22 Feb 1882 in Philadelphia, Pennsylvania,

---

[20]Obituary of Dorothy A. Kinniburgh, 4 April 2004, Sunday, *Chicago Tribune*, Chicago, Illinois, <<www.newspapers.com>>, downloaded 30 June 2018.

[21]Obituary of William M. Rowe, Jr., 10 May 2012, Colonial Chapel Funeral Home & Crematory, 15525 South 73rd Avenue, Orland Park, Illinois 60462, <<www.ancestry.com>>, 30 June 2018.

father: Thomas (sic) Killeen, mother: Anna McPherson.[22]

    b.   Dorothy Allan (sic) Rowe Kinniburgh, born: 27 May 1912 in Philadelphia, Pennsylvania, father: William M. Rowe (sic), mother: Lillian Killeen.[23]

DISCUSSION:

The research amply supports the hypothesis that the first wife and the daughter of John Thomas Smith were named Lillian Killeen and Dorothy Allen Smith, respectively. The records that support this finding include:

    a.   The 1903 marriage record of the John Thomas Smith and Lillian Killeen.[24]

    b.   The 1906 birth record of their son James Allen Smith.[25]

    c.   The 1906 baptismal record of their son, James Allen Smith.[26]

    d.   The 1911 death record of their son, James Allen Smith.[27]

    e.   The 1912 birth record of their daughter, Dorothy Allen Smith.[28]

---

[22]Lillian Killeen Rowe, Social Security Application and Claims Index, 1936-2007, <<www.ancestry.com>>, downloaded 30 May 2018.

[23]Dorothy Allan (sic) Rowe Kinniburgh, Social Security Application and Claims Index, 1936-2007, <<www.ancestry.com>>, downloaded 30 May 2018.

[24]Affidavit of Applicant for Marriage License [with Return], # 164419, 1 August 1903, (John T. Smith & Lillian Killeen), Philadelphia, Pennsylvania Civil Marriages, 1677-1950, <<www.familysearch.org>>, downloaded 28 May 2018.

[25]Birth Certificate of James Allen Smith, 14 January 1906, Philadelphia, Pennsylvania, Pennsylvania, Birth Certificates, 1906-1910, <<www.ancestry.com>>, downloaded 30 June 2018.

[26]Baptism of John Allen Smith, 23 December 1906, All Saints Episcopal Church, Philadelphia, Pennsylvania, Pennsylvania and New Jersey Church and Town Records, 1669-2013, <<www.ancestry.com>>, downloaded 1 July 2018.

[27]Death Certificate of James A. Smith, 10 April 1911, Philadelphia, Pennsylvania, Pennsylvania Death Certificates, 1906-1966, <<www.ancestry.com>>, downloaded 1 July 2018.

[28]Birth Certificate of Dorothy Allen Smith, 27 May 1912, Philadelphia, Pennsylvania, Pennsylvania State Archives, Harrisburg, Pennsylvania 17120-0090.

The research also revealed that John Thomas Smith and Lillian (Killeen) Smith were divorced on 19 January 1914.[29] Additional research to determine what happened to Lillian (Killeen) Smith after her divorce from John Thomas Smith, revealed that she married William Matthew Rowe in Camden, New Jersey, on 17 August 1914.[30]

Further research revealed a baptismal record that states William and Lillian Rowe baptized a child named Dorothy Allan (sic) Rowe at Saint James the Less Episcopal Church in Philadelphia, Pennsylvania, on 5 June 1915.[31] The baptismal record states that Dorothy Allan (sic) Rowe was born 27 May 1912 which is consistent with the birth date contained in the birth certificate of Dorothy Allen Smith, the daughter of John T. Smith and Lily Killen (sic).[32] The baptized child is, therefore, believed to be the biological daughter of John Thomas Smith and not of William Rowe.[33]

Five years after the baptism, Lillian (Killeen) Rowe and her daughter, Dorothy Allan Rowe, were enumerated living in Chicago, Cook County, Illinois, in the household of William Rowe.[34] In 1930, they were both enumerated in Broadview, Cook County, Illinois.[35] According to the obituary of Lillian (Killen) Rowe, she was still living in Broadview at the time of her death

---

[29]Affidavit of Applicant for Marriage License [with Return], # 520445, 22 October 1925, (John Smith & Margaret McCauley), Philadelphia, Pennsylvania Civil Marriages, 1677-1950, <<www.familysearch.org>>, downloaded 28 June 2018.

[30]Certificate and Record of Marriage of William M. Rowe and Lillian Killeen dated 17 August 1914, New Jersey State Archives, P.O. Box 307, Trenton, NJ 08625-0307.

[31]Baptism of Dorothy Allan (sic) Rowe, 5 June 1915, Saint James the Less Episcopal Church, Philadelphia, Pennsylvania, Pennsylvania and New Jersey Church and Town Records, 1669-2013, <<www.ancestry.com>>, downloaded 30 May 2018.

[32]Birth Certificate of Dorothy Allen Smith, 27 May 1912, Philadelphia, Pennsylvania, Pennsylvania State Archives, Harrisburg, Pennsylvania 17120-0090.

[33]This finding assumes there was *not* an extra-marital relationship between Lillian (Killeen) Smith and William Rowe prior to 27 May 1912. DNA testing to confirm paternity is *not* possible because there are no known living descendants of either John Thomas Smith or Dorothy Allan Rowe.

[34]1920 U.S. Census (population), Illinois, Cook County, Chicago, Ward 23, E.D. 1257, page 6A, National Archives Microfilm Publication T625, Roll 333, Household of William Rowe.

[35]1930 U.S. Census (population), Illinois, Cook County, Broadview, E.D. 2299, page 4B, National Archives Microfilm Publication T626, Roll 506, Household of William Rowe.

in 1968.[36] Her daughter, Dorothy Allan (Rowe) Kinniburgh, was also living in Broadview at the time of her death in 2004.[37]

There was an inconsistency in two records created by Lillian (Killeen) Rowe after her divorce from John Thomas Smith concerning the first name of her father. Her 1914 marriage record to William M. Rowe states that her father's name was *John* Killeen whereas her SSCI record states that her father's name was *Thomas* Killeen. The SSCI record is believed to be in error. This finding is supported by the death certificate of Lillian Rowe which states that her parents were John Killeen and Annie McPherson.[38] Lillian (Killeen) Rowe's parents died when she was very young. Her father, John Killeen, died on 6 April 1882 (the year she was born) and her mother, Anna (McPherson) Killeen, died on 8 October 1886 when she was only about 4 years old.[39,40] Her only sibling, a brother named Thomas Killeen, died on 11 May 1937.[41] It is reasonable to surmise that Lillian (Killeen) Rowe may simply have made a mistake regarding her father's first name when she completed her social security paperwork.

As a result of the correlation and compilation of the evidence, a descendant chart was created for Lillian (Killeen) Smith Rowe (see Exhibit A). The descendant chart shows that she was married twice and had three children; a son and a daughter during her first marriage and a son during her second marriage.

---

[36]Obituary of Lillian Rowe, 25 September 1968, Wednesday, *Chicago Tribune*, Chicago, Illinois, <<www.newspapers.com>>, downloaded 30 May 2018.

[37]Obituary of Dorothy A. Kinniburgh, 4 April 2004, Sunday, *Chicago Tribune*, Chicago, Illinois, <<www.newspapers.com>>, downloaded 30 June 2018.

[38]Death Certificate of Lillian Rowe, 24 September 1968, Cook County, Illinois, Illinois Department of Public Health, Springfield, Illinois 62702-2737.

[39]Return of a Death in the City of Philadelphia for John Killeen, Philadelphia City Death Certificates, 1803-1915, <<www.familysearch.org>>, downloaded 5 June 2018.

[40]Return of a Death in the City of Philadelphia for Annie Killeen, Philadelphia City Death Certificates, 1803-1915, <<www.familysearch.org>>, downloaded 5 June 2018.

[41]Death Certificate of Thomas Killeen, 11 May 1937, Crafton, Allegheny County, Pennsylvania, Pennsylvania Death Certificates, 1906-1966, <<www.ancestry.com>>, downloaded 5 June 2018 states the names of his parents were: John Killeen and Annie MacPherson (sic).

CONCLUSION:

The evidence supports the conclusion that the Lillian Killeen who married John Thomas Smith in 1903 and William Matthew Rowe in 1914 are the same person. The evidence also supports the conclusion that the daughter of John Thomas Smith who visited him and his second wife, Margaret McCauley, in Philadelphia for a few days in the 1930s was Dorothy Allen Smith, later known as Dorothy Allan (sic) Rowe, who married James Kinniburgh.

Descendant Chart for
Lillian Killeen

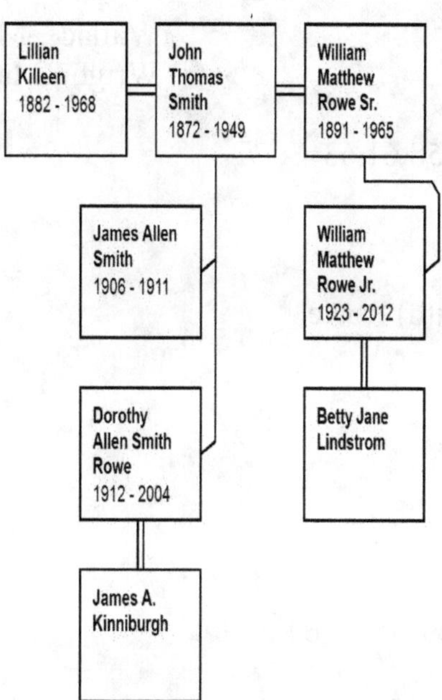

EXHIBIT A

65   Appendix F

Willis Skillman McCauley, Sr.
1896-1970

Willis Skillman McCauley, Sr., was the only surviving son of Thomas and Mary Ann (Wallace) McCauley. He was born September 8, 1896 in Philadelphia. He was named after the Rev. Willis B. Skillman, pastor of Tabor Presbyterian Church. He was also a veteran of World War I having served in the U.S. Marine Corps as a private from June 29, 1917 to March 31, 1919. He was honorably discharged at Fort Mifflin, Pennsylvania.

After World War I, he worked as a "board boy" for Cassatt & Company, a Philadelphia-based investment banking and brokerage firm, marking up-to-date information on stock quotation boards and later he worked for them as a bookkeeper. When Cassatt & Company was bought by Merrill Lynch in1940, he lost his job and ended up as a guard at the First Pennsylvania Banking & Trust Company. He got the job as a guard through a friend who had been in the U.S. Marine Corps with him in World War I where they had been assigned to the military police.

He married Mae Schwartz. They had one son, Willis Skillman "Skill" McCauley, Jr.

Willis S. McCauley, Sr.

Willis & Mae McCauley

Willis S. McCauley, Jr.

******

On May 30, 2000, Willis Skillman McCauley, Jr., provided the following recollections about his parents and himself.

My mother, Mae Schwartz, was born on February 18, 1892 in Philadelphia. Before she married my father, she was the supervisor of 5 girls at an auto insurance company located at 5th and Spruce. One of the girls who worked there decided to give a party. The girl lived at 58th and Chester Avenue. My mother was invited to attend the party by the girl who worked in her office and Aunt Marge McCauley was invited to attend the party by that girl's sister. Aunt Marge was asked to bring her brother. So, that's how my parents met.

My parents were married in Elkton, Maryland, on January 30, 1921. I was born January 13, 1922 at the home of my maternal grandmother who lived at 2353 E. Firth Street near the Delaware River. Soon after I was born, we moved in with Aunt Marge at 1606 S. 53rd Street. After 11 months, we moved a block away to 1503 S. Lindenwood Street which is where I grew up. I was baptized at Tabor Presbyterian Church in 1922. I attended B.B. Comegys Grammar School, Shaw Junior High School and West Philadelphia High School where I graduated in early 1940, January or February.

Around 1934, my father applied for veteran's compensation based on his World War I service. I think he received about $200.00. He bought a Model A Ford. He used to drive Uncle John around in that car when Uncle John went to collect insurance premiums from his clients and rent from his tenants. Uncle John was a good man. He was also an insurance salesman and he owned some houses or an apartment in Philadelphia. He helped my father pay off our mortgage at 1503 S. Lindenwood Street when my father couldn't pay anymore during the Depression. If it hadn't been for Uncle John we would have lost the house

After graduation from high school, I went to work for the Fidelity Philadelphia Trust Company where I worked in trust securities. In 1942, with the advent of World War II, I went into the military. I was on active duty in the United States Army until 1946. I served in both Europe and Japan. I came back from Japan and was discharged at Fort Dix, New Jersey, in 1946.

Once I got back home, my mother asked me to start going to the Catholic church with them. So, to make peace, I went to Most Blessed Sacrament and found that there was a new priest. I told him I had been baptized at Tabor Presbyterian Church. He said that if I had proof of my baptism it would not be necessary to re-baptize me. I didn't have any proof at the time so the priest gave me a conditional baptism. That's how it happened in 1946 and my mother was very much pleased that we were all attending the same church together.

After I returned home, I went to Temple University as an undergraduate on the G.I. bill and I majored in accounting & pre-law. I graduated in 1948. Then I went to Temple University Law School and graduated in 1953. From 1953 to 1958, I worked for the State of Pennsylvania Unemployment Office. I went to work for the Social Security Administration in 1958. I worked there for 23 years before retiring in 1982.

My father's date of birth was September 8, 1896. He died on September 10, 1970 in Philadelphia. We published an obituary and a death notice for him in the *Philadelphia Inquirer*, but the obituary has errors in it about his work history. He was actually a bookkeeper when he

worked at the brokerage firm. He didn't start working as a watchman until 1940 after his job at
the brokerage firm ended.

About two years after my father died, about 1973, my mother and I moved to 643 E.
Rector Street in Roxborough which was near where my mother's sister's daughter named Little
Gertie [i.e., Gertrude Mary (Erl) Newell] and her children lived. We were very happy there.

My mother died on July 28, 1982. I put her death notice in the *Philadelphia Inquirer*,
too.

After my mother died, I stopped going to the Roman Catholic church. That's about the
time I began listening to Harold Camping on the radio at night and heard the whole story about
John Calvin, John Knox, and Martin Luther and I bought two books on Martin Luther. [i.e.,
Harold Camping, founder and head of Family Stations Inc., otherwise known as "Family Radio,"
was for many years a Calvinistic radio Bible teacher.] I got real educated on the subject. After
my mother died, a neighbor named Ammie Tippett sold me a ticket to a dinner at Grace Lutheran
Church. I attended the dinner, went to some of the services, and then bought a ticket to another
dinner in the Fall. It was in December 1982 that I received the Reaffirmation Rite at Grace
Lutheran Church in Roxborough in the belief that it was a Reformed church, but that turned out

to be incorrect because the church was not affiliated with the Missouri Synod Lutheran Church.

In 1994, I moved to a studio apartment at the Peter Becker Community which is affiliated with the German Brethren (not Mennonite) church. I did not join the Brethren church. I mentally rejoined the Presbyterian church. At first I was able to attend Presbyterian services at the Peter Becker Community because a local Presbyterian congregation used the facility until they obtained a church of their own about a half mile away. Now I listen to Presbyterian services on the radio early on Sunday morning and then I attend Brethren services at 11 AM at the Peter Becker Community. Brethren services are similar to Presbyterian services. Until recently, the Presbyterian services that I listened to on the radio were conducted by John Montgomery Boyce of Tenth Presbyterian located at 23rd and Spruce, but Mr. Boyce died in the Fall of 1999.

I plan to be buried at Saints Peter and Paul Cemetery in Broomall in the same plot as my parents. I made the arrangements through the Turner Funeral Home while I was still attending Grace Lutheran Church. The funeral home called the cemetery and the cemetery said okay because I was attending a Lutheran church and they recognized Lutherans. So, the Lord will take me to Heaven from Saints Peter and Paul Cemetery.

******

Willis Skillman McCauley, Jr., died on November 4, 2002, at the Peter Becker Community. He was not buried in the same plot with his parents because he had prepaid his funeral expenses and the funeral home claimed that he had called them in the months before he died and directed them not to bury him at Saints Peter and Paul Cemetery. Instead, the funeral home had him buried at Ivy Hill Cemetery.

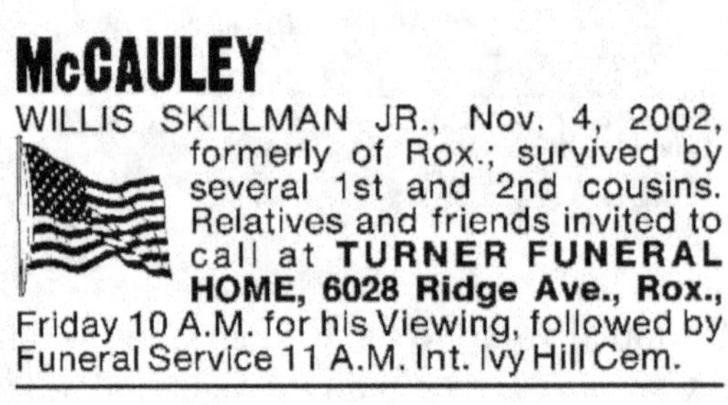

Shortly before his death, Willis Skillman McCauley, Jr., agreed to be interviewed for the Library of Congress Veterans History Project about his World War II experience. The complete text of his oral interview as contained in the Willis Skillman McCauley, Jr. Collection is presented herewith.

Willis Skillman McCauley, Jr. Collection
Veterans History Project
Library of Congress
March 24, 2002

The Library of Congress >> American Folklife Center

Home » Search Results » Full Description

Print   Subscribe   Share/Save

Willis Skillman McCauley, Jr. Collection

Biographical Information

Name:
Willis Skillman McCauley, Jr.
State of Birth:
PA

Gender
Male
Race
Unspecified

War or Conflict
World War, 1939-1945
Military Status
Veteran
Dates of Service
1942-1946
Entrance into Service
Enlisted
Branch of Service
Army
Unit of Service
97th Infantry Division, 387th Regiment
Location of Service
Fort Meade, Maryland; Joplin, Missouri; Amarillo, Texas;
Springfield, Missouri; France; Germany; Fort Bragg,
North Carolina; Fort Lewis, Washington; Tokyo and Ota,
Japan; Philippines
Battles/Campaigns
Düsseldorf
Highest Rank
Private First Class
Prisoner of War
Unknown

Collection Information

Type of Resource:
Audio: Microcassette [1 item] -- Oral history interview
Manuscript: Creative works [3 items] -- Typewritten
document
Manuscript: Transcript [item] -- Transcription of audio
recording
Manuscript: Regimental/unit histories [1 item] -- Mixed
(handwritten and typewritten documents)
Photograph: Original photographic print [20 items] --
Photographs
Artifact: Artifact [2 items] -- Other
Interviewer:
Kathryn Torpey
Contributor:
Kathryn Torpey
Collection #:
AFC/2001/001/18180
Subjects:
McCauley Jr., Willis Skillman
World War, 1939-1945--Personal Narratives
United States. Army.
Cite as:
Willis Skillman McCauley, Jr. Collection
(AFC/2001/001/18180), Veterans History Project,
American Folklife Center, Library of Congress

Last Edit: 2016-01-19

XML: MODS Bibliographic Data | METS Object Description

Home » Search Results » **Full Description**

Segment 1: For The Record

This recording is being made on March 24, 2002, at the Peter Becker Community, 265 Ridgeview Estates, Harleysville, Pennsylvania, the residence of Willis Skillman McCauley, Jr., who is being interviewed by his cousin, Kathryn Chambers Torpey.

Question: For the record, what branch of the service did you serve in?

Answer: I was in the Army. I served in the 97th Infantry Division, 387th Regiment.

Question: Which war did you serve in?

Answer: I served in World War II.

Question: What rank where you?

Answer: I was a PFC, a Private First Class.

Question: Where did you serve?

Answer: I served in both Europe and in Japan.

Segment 2: Jogging the Memory

Question: You were born and grew up in Philadelphia. What did you do after you graduated from high school in January of 1940?

Answer: After I graduated from West Philadelphia high school I went to work for the Fidelity Philadelphia Trust Company. That was a bank. I worked in trust securities.

Question: After the war started were you drafted or did you enlist?

Answer: In 1942 I joined the Signal Corps Reserves.

Question: What happened after that?

Answer: In 1943, April of 1943 about six months after I joined the reserves I was activated and I was sent to Fort Meade, Maryland, for training. Then I was sent to Joplin Missouri. I was in the infantry in Joplin. While I was there I took a psychomotor test. And after that test they said I was classified as an navigator so I was sent to an Army Air Corps installation in Amarillo Texas for training. From Amarillo I was sent to Drake University in Iowa. I was an aviation cadet and I was in pre

flight training. The problem was so many US soldiers, Army soldiers, were killed
or wounded in Italy that there was a manpower shortage in the infantry so in 1944
I and all of my fellow trainees were transferred back to infantry units. I was sent
to Springfield Missouri. That's where I was assigned to the 97th Infantry Division
the 387th Regiment as a Private First Class.

Segment 3: Experiences

Question: When you were sent to Europe, where exactly did you go?

Answer: In February 1945 we went to France. After we got there we were put on trains in
box cars all of us and we all traveled across France and Belgium and a little sliver
of Holland on the train. When we got off the train we traveled in a convoy of 2 ½
ton trucks. They were called deuce and a halfs. I was in the back of one of the
trucks.

Question: Did you know where you are going?

Answer: Not exactly. I know we went through the city of Aachen in Germany about
midnight. I looked out the back of the truck. I thought I was looking at the scene
from a horror movie. The whole place had been devastated and demolished by the
Air Force. Aachen was like a scene from hell.

Question: What happened after that?

Answer: When we finally got to the West Bank of the Rhine River we couldn't get across
because the German soldiers on the East Bank were firing too fiercely. So we
went down the Rhine River on the West Bank to the city of Cologne. I remember
I saw a sign in German that said something like KOLN - four letters. Near there,
the engineers made a bridge by lashing boats together on the river. The river was
running really fast. They put a bridge surface over the top of the boats and we
drove across the bridge. That's how the infantry crossed the Rhine River at
Cologne. Great job.

Question: Did you stay in Cologne?

Answer: No. Once we got back on land on the other side we made a left turn by a big
Cathedral and went into the Ruhr Valley. From there we went to Dusseldorf,
Germany, and finished up fighting there sometime in April. After we left
Dusseldorf we went across Central Germany until we got to the border of
Czechoslovakia. We went may be 15 or 20 miles into Czechoslovakia to the town
of Plzen. That's where we were on May 8, 1945, when Germany surrendered.
That's where we were on VE Day.

Question: What happened to you after Germany surrendered?

Answer: Well, we had hoped that we were going to stay there, but immediately we were
               sent back to the United States to Fort Bragg, North Carolina. From there we were
               sent to Fort Was..., Fort Lewis in Washington State to get ready for the invasion
               of Japan.

Question: Then what happened?

Answer: I remember we were put on board the troop ship, U.S.S. Kenton a 10,000 ton
               Navy ship. That's where we were when the bomb was dropped on Hiroshima on
               August 15, 1945. Another bomb was dropped on Nagasaki about a week later.
               That was VJ Day, but we kept on going and finally arrived in Tokyo Bay where a
               Japanese man came on our ship and took over from the captain. He was a pilot
               who guided our ship inside the sea wall to the port. From Tokyo I was sent to the
               city of Ota. I stayed there for six months.   I was a messenger with a Jeep. I took
               messages back and forth to the officers.

Question: Were you awarded any medals or citations?

Answer: They said we were supposed to get credit for one battle star which was called the
               Campaign Germany or maybe the Central Europe Campaign. We might have
               gotten one for the Rhineland Campaign too and one for the occupation of Japan.
               I'm not sure any more.

Segment 4: Life

Question: Do you have photographs?

Answer: Yes. I have a lot of photographs. You know, like here is what I think is the most
               interesting one even though it's not very clear. Sometime in the winter right
               before Christmas of 1945 a bunch of us went down to Hiroshima where the bomb
               was dropped and we took pictures and, boy, there's nothing left. It's, just about
               everything is gone. And I have pictures of the air[plane] factory where we pulled
               duty. It was an airplane factory at Ota where I was stationed and they built planes
               there during the war and we were charged with helping to see that they were
               destroyed after the war. And there are several pictures some with just the planes
               themselves and others with various members of the unit in it. In addition, I have
               one here that talks about welcoming us, welcoming all visitors, to the 387th
               Infantry Regiment and gives the speed limits for the vehicles. There's a lot of
               pictures that we took of the people - just little boys, little girls, men and women,
               you know, on the streets and in the town - quite a few of those pictures. Pictures
               of the farm land and the mountains in the distance from Ota. There's a, oh and I

forgot about we have pictures of Leyte Bay in the Philippines and they were taken sometime in the latter part of 1945. Ah, there's a picture of Yokohama that I have here, two of them I think, and several pictures of Tokyo Bay late 1945, early 1946.

Question: You also have here something that looks like an insignia. What it is exactly?

Answer: Oh, this is the unit patch of the 97th Infantry Division. It's called the Trident and this was for the entire Division. My unit was the 387th Infantry Division (sic), Infantry Regiment, that was part of that Division.

Question: Finally, you have some kind of sign here. It looks like you were trying to catch a train and it's partly in Japanese. What's that all about?

Answer: Oh, that's when a group of us went from Ota where we were stationed to downtown Tokyo to see this museum and we got the Japanese who were working there to write it out in Japanese as well as in English so we could follow the correct itinerary on the railroad. Somewhere on here I remember it tells us what gate to go into in the museum so we could get to the part that we were primarily interested in and I don't see it anymore, but I know it was there because we went in the gate at the two gargoyle type statues right there on either side of the gate and they told us that's the one we were to go into, so that's the one we went into.

Question: Do you have anything else on the pictures that you want to tell about ro is that it?

Answer: That's generally it. I mean there's a lot... I could go through the pictures and, you know, show details, here's a picture of me with another guy I don't even remember his name now. Oh, I forgot about this, they tried to teach me how to ski over there and this is me on a pair of skis up in the mountains away from Ota and fortunately the grounhd looks flat because I was terrified. I knew that I was never going to be a skier. If you look you can see that I am extremely nervous about being on these skis. And, I guess, the last one is, here's the entrance to out mess hall and this was probably for either Christmas Day or Thanksgiving Day in 1945 because they're serving turkey and giblet gravy and mashed potatoes and all the things that you would get with a traditional Thanksgiving dinner. And, neither one of the two guys in the picture is me, but I don't remember who they are.

Segment 5: After Service

Question: When did you get back home?

Answer: I arrived back in San Francisco on March 21, 1946, on board the troop ship the U.S.S. General Blatchford. From there I took a train to, it was all the way across the country, to Fort Dix, New Jersey, where I was discharged from the service.

Question: After the service did you work or go back to school?

Answer: I went to college on the GI Bill. I attended Temple University in North
                Philadelphia as an undergraduate and I majored in accounting and pre-law. I
                graduated from there in 1948. Then I went at Temple University Law School. I
                graduated from Law School in 1953.

Segment 6: Later Years and Closing

Question: What did you go on to do as a career after the war?

Answer: From 1953 to 1958 I worked for the State of Pennsylvania Unemployment
                Compensation Office. In 1958, I went to work for the Social Security
                Administration. I worked there for 23 years. I retired in 1982.

Question: Did your military experience influence your thinking about war or about the
                military in general?

Answer: Oh yes. As I said before I was on board the troop ship, the U.S.S. Kenton on the
                day the bomb was dropped on Hiroshima. I was on my way to be a part of
                the invasion of Japan. Instead I became part of the occupation in Japan. That was
                a big difference.

Question: How did your service and experiences affect your life?

Answer: I became a much more religious person. I became a student of religion. I have
                studied the Catholic faith, the Presbyterian faith, and the Lutheran faith. I have
                even written poetry about my faith. It's a central focus of my life. I listen to the
                Presbyterian services on the radio early on Sunday morning and I attend the
                Brethren services at 11:00 AM here where I live.

Question: Is there anything you would like to add that we haven't covered already in this
                interview?

Answer: Yes. I would like to say special thanks are due to my aunt Mary McCauley
                Chambers that's your grandmother, and my aunt Marge McCauley Smith because
                they got me involved with the Presbyterian Church when I was six years old. I
                went to Sunday School at the Presbyterian Church because of them. I had
                fourteen years of medals for attending Sunday School. The medal for the first year
                was a central medal with the cross. The medal for the second year was a wreath.
                The medals for the rest of the years were bars. I don't know where those medals
                are anymore.

                    Appendix G

Okay, thank you very much for your time. I appreciate the interview.

It's been my pleasure.

Note: All original photographic prints referenced in this interview [20 items] are part of the
Willis Skillman McCauley, Jr. Collection at the Library of Congress.

Source Citation:
Willis Skillman McCauley, Jr. Collection
(AFC/2001/001/18180), Veterans History Project,
American Folklife Center, Library of Congress

* * * * * * * *

The Reformation - God's Alteration   *By W.S.M.*

Reformation, Reformation!
A word that shocked many a nation.
Seize that Saxon Luther, they cried,
After reading his Theses Ninety-Five
Posted on the church door at Wittenberg
Where at long last the truth would be heard.
  It was in October of Fifteen-Seventeen
  That an obscure monk would be heard and seen,
  When at first he contended with indulgences
  And denied the power of the church's consequences.
  Since the Scripture did not support this belief
  Removal of such a tradition brought blessed relief.
    How was mankind to be saved
    And how would the way of the lost be paved.
    The Church said it had this authority
    But Luther rejected their priority.
    He prayed for its faith that the Church would see
    And stood at Worms and quietly sighed, "God help me.

So Reform at last had really begun, And the church suprised would be on the run.
But this would be a long hard fight, And the outcome at first did not look bright.
Although the Bishop of Rome at his keys did nod, Martin Luther found faith and grace
from God.
  A Holy Priesthood of all believers became so clear, That no longer any class of men
  do we need to fear.
  For now in Heaven stands our Eternal High Priest, Jesus, the Christ, who calls us to
  His Father's feast.
  For the truth from the Apostles had been revealed, And Luther did not want these
  concepts concealed.
    The Empire tried to stop him at Spires, But Luther's friends made known their desires.
    For they wanted to reform this Ancient Church, Which had fallen in time to such a
    reproach.
    Back and forth their arguments raged, The Church was adamant, nothing was changed.
    The German Princes rebelled and took their stance, And this New Movement was
    called, "The Protestants."
Luther saw the condition of the human race, And their trust in merits to win a heavenly
place.
He knew all their deeds would be in vain, For the Scriptures show the way so plain.
The Church must shed some old traditions, And allow reform of present conditions.
  The Reformation has done its work quite well, And now we see God's grace through his
  Gospel.
  For none of our works can please the Lord, But saved we are by faith alone in His word.
  So thanks to those Reformers who were so fine, That for the Bible they put their
  lives on the line.
  Our eyes have been opened by the Reformation, Praise God for His gift of Eternal
  Salvation.

* * * * * * * *

"For The Love Of You And Me"

IF, I could take some people back   Back in time on a railroad track
Before the Reformation   And the birth of many a nation
Back for nineteen centuries   To the time of Roman glory
So that we may re-live   The world's greatest story
When mankind was saved   And would live forever more
The ride will seem quite long   And be full of many fears
But along with some song   There may be some tears
We sit back and wait very patiently As time moves backward so constantly
Finally the years have all rolled away   And now in the morning's light
Begins a meaningful new day   For there on the horizon
As we draw near   Three wooden crosses stand out so clear
Now we can see the middle one   Where our Savior was hung
And cursed on this tree   For the likes of you and me
At Calvary, at Calvary

Our train stops at a nearby station   And we get out to visit this location
The event we are told is several days old   And that while nailed to
His cross
There was darkness at noon   And with lightning and thunder
The heavens did toss   And the ground they said did violently shake
As God's wrath against man   The Lord Jesus did willingly take
So the Savior suffered and for us He died   And His forgiveness for us
He did not hide
Then mercy and grace came down to stay   And our sin debt was paid on
that awesome day
His body was taken down so reverently   And sealed in this tomb very
recently
But there we behold   No stone at the door!
How can this be   We earnestly implore
Then down in our hearts these words we hear: Why seek ye the living
among the dead
My Son is not here, He has arisen instead   So be of good cheer and put
away your fear
For now you know of My great love   And the truth which I did promise
thee
That Satan's captives would go free   If on My Son, the Christ, you *did*
believe
For by my grace salvation has been assured   And through faith alone you
rest secured
For where I am, you shall forever be   Behold-death has now lost it's
sting
            And the grave it's victory
            All because of Jesus
            And what He did, eternally,
            For the love of you and me
            At Calvary, at Calvary.

                    Willis S. Mc Cauley
                    ****

For God so loved the world, that he
gave his only begotten Son, that
whosoever believeth in him should not
perish, but have everlasting life.

                    -John 3:16

79   Appendix G

Mary Ann (McCauley) Chambers
1892-1984

Mary Ann (McCauley) Chambers, the youngest surviving daughter of Thomas and Mary Ann (Wallace) McCauley, was born July 7, 1892 in Philadelphia. She was baptized at Tabor Presbyterian Church. Much like her older sister, she left school at age 16 to work as a telephone operator for the Bell Telephone Company of Pennsylvania in order to help support the family.

In July 2000, her older son, William Scott Chambers provided the following recollections about his mother and family life in West Philadelphia when he was a child.

******

My parents were married on July 30, 1918 by the Rev. Freeman D. Bovard, a Methodist Episcopal minister. They were married the minister's house located at 51st and Greenway Avenue in West Philadelphia. They didn't have a formal wedding ceremony because my father was a fireman in the U.S. Navy during World War I. He had come down to Philadelphia from New York where his ship had come into port during World War I.

Pauline and Fred Queroli, their best friends, and John Smith, who later married Aunt Marge, went with them while my grandfather, Thomas McCauley, stayed home to cook the supper for everyone. No doubt it was a happy day for my mother and father.

My father, Henry Grafe Chambers, was born January 8, 1897. He was 5 years younger than my mother which was somewhat of an embarrassment to her so she was always vague about the year she was born.

I was born February 25, 1921 at the Presbyterian Hospital in Philadelphia which was unusual in those days when most children were born at home. At the time, my parents were probably living at 1631 S. 53rd Street. My mother told me it was a difficult birth. I was badly banged up by the use of forceps that crushed part of my scull resulting in partial paralysis on my right side. We both almost died.

My brother Thomas Wallace Chambers was born at home on March 25, 1923, with no apparent complications, while we were living at 1547 S. Lindenwood Street. As was the custom in those days, he was named after his maternal grandfather. He was in the U.S. Army Air Corps in World War II. He survived a mid-air collision during the war via an emergency parachute jump on July 8, 1944 over Rutland County, England. He fell 700 feet, pulled the cord at 200 feet, and the parachute opened at 45 feet. The vicar of the village where he was found after the parachute drop wrote a letter to my mother describing the entire event which he witnessed from the ground. Reportedly, it was a beautiful letter. After World War II, my brother was accepted as an Air Force Cadet. In July 1948, he was to go to Randolph, Texas by train for training as a pilot. Everyone including his fiancee, Florence Clark took him to the Philadelphia train station. After the train left the station, Florence told my parents that she and Tom were secretly married.

As a child, I was called Bill or Billy. My mother was called Mary, my father was called Harry, and my brother was called Tom. No other nicknames.

Tom Chambers
U.S. Army Air Corps

Bill Chambers
U.S. Merchant Marine

My father was a fireman and an engineer on the Pennsylvania Railroad which he joined in 1916. He was promoted to Road Foreman of Engines on the Pennsylvania Reading Seashore Line in 1942. My mother did not work outside the home after she was married.

From the time I was born until I was 20 we always lived in West Philadelphia. First, we lived at 1631 S. 53rd Street and later a block away at 1547 S. Lindenwood Street at the opposite end of the street from my first cousin, Skill McCauley. Our house at 1547 S. Lindenwood Street was a two-story, three bedroom, row house. I remember my father figuring out that there were 57 children living on the street in 48 houses. We never did stay overnight with a friend. There weren't many houses on Lindenwood Street that had any room for guests.

My bedroom was on the second floor in the rear. I had it all to myself. Tom was in the middle room. I had a single bed, Morris chair, antique chest, and closet. It was hot. No air conditioning. Cats used to fight all night in the summer in the back alleys and yards. When I was young, it was a regular event to catch a mouse in the house several times a year. We set traps quite regularly.   We were also about the only family or one of the few families on our street to have a telephone in the 1930's. Some of our close neighbors could use our telephone and put a nickel in the tin can by the telephone.

I only have vague memories of my maternal grandfather, Thomas McCauley, walking on his crutches as he only had one leg. I remember that in my early youth my mother suffered a complicated miscarriage and surgery requiring a lengthy hospital stay. During that time, my brother lived with Aunt Marge (McCauley) Smith and I lived around the corner at 5313 Yocum Street for about a month with my paternal grandmother, Josephine (Reitze) Chambers. I always remembered this stay as a very pleasant experience.

I only had one aunt and her name was Margaret (McCauley) Smith. She was my mother's older sister. My brother and I were very fond of her. We called her Aunt Marge. She was amusing and nice. Quite funny, really, though often unintentionally. She lived on the next street to us (1606 S. 53rd Street) and we saw her often. My mother was living with Aunt Marge when Aunt Marge died at home on 53rd Street in 1957.

I only had one uncle and his name was Willis Skillman McCauley. He was my mother's younger brother. He and his family lived on the same street with us. He owned a 1929 Ford Model A. During the 1930's, we took many Sunday afternoon drives with them which was the custom in those days. Our first car was a 1936 Plymouth.

When we were children, I remember that my first cousin, Josephine Thompson, used to ride me around the neighborhood on the back of her bike. She had a small cushion for me to sit on over the rear fender of her bike. Neither my brother nor I ever had a bike (small tricycles, yes). My mother never approved of them. She felt they were dangerous in the city and that was that.

I also remember that I rode medium-sized ponies a great deal when I was a kid. A stable near me took the ponies out to sell rides in the neighborhoods. My brother and I and a few other kids would ride the ponies with the owners when they went to sell the rides and we would also walk the ponies with the little kids in the saddles. We didn't get paid for any of this work. The ponies were mostly from Chincoteague with a few Shetlands thrown in.

When I was seven and my brother was five, my father put us in a small open cockpit biplane that landed on the beach at Wildwood Crest in New Jersey. When we returned he put my first cousin, Josephine Thompson on biplane. The airplane had two cockpits. The rear one for the pilot and the front one was for the passenger or two kids. When we got back home my mother and my grandmother gave my father Hell. This was a big adventure in 1928.

Whenever we got in trouble my mother would come after us and wack us with the first thing she could grab, frying pan, stick, switch. I bagged school occasionally and usually got caught. Punishment was fairly severe. I was usually restricted to the house for a week or more.

When I was born, Woodrow Wilson was the President. He only had one month left in his term. After that, Warren Harding was President. My mother was a staunch Republican. My father never said much about politics, but I know he voted for FDR in 1936. The same with my paternal grandparents.

When I was a child, I can remember a number of snow storms closing down Lindenwood Street to traffic. I also have vivid memories of the draft horses falling on the ice and snow. When we were children, everyone had a sled including my brother and me. We also built snowmen. We used pieces of coal for the face and sticks for the arms. I rarely went ice skating in the winter, but I did have a leg go through the ice up to my thigh. The temperature was two degrees and I had to walk 2 miles or more to get home. While the snow was often deep, at least for children, the schools were seldom closed. The schools were close and everyone walked to school. The main streets with trolley cars were cleared by trolley car plows, but otherwise there were no plows. The side streets remained partially blocked except for a center opening made by neighbors for horse drawn delivery of milk and bread and pick up wagons for garbage, ashes, and trash.

My favorite meal as a child was hot cakes and sausage for any meal. Since my father was often away, my brother and I had this often for supper. Strange as it may seem, I always remember supper at 5:00 PM with my brother and mother. In fact, the number one curfew was to be home for supper at 5:00 PM. No excuses. When we were younger we were not allowed out after dark. As we got older, my mother changed the rules from time to time, but they were strict. We always had a good dessert. My father was not often home for supper when we were kids. The only type of food I can remember making was scrambled eggs and scrapple.

How we spent our Saturdays during the school year depended on the season. We played baseball or football (no basketball). We also played hockey or skated long distances all over West Philadelphia. In fact, Tom and I both had roller skates and roamed all over southwest Philadelphia and played hockey on the street. I recall my mother (on a dare I guess) putting on my roller skates and skating up and down the street with the boys. She was a big hit. We walked and roamed everywhere. We also explored undeveloped areas and swampy wetlands (meadows) along the Pennsylvania Railroad.

When we were kids, it was customary for every boy to tie a string around a loose tooth and walk around with the string hanging down until he got the courage to yank the tooth out.

My favorite movies were the Saturday afternoon serials with cowboys Buck Jones, Tim McCoy, Tom Tyler. In fact, my favorite movie stars were the cowboys Tim McCoy and Tom Tyler. We also saw Dracula several times and my first cousin, Skill McCauley, always ducked under the seat in the spooky parts. The scary movies of the time - Dracula, The Phantom of the Opera, The Terror, Frankenstein, etc., used to keep me awake at night. As a small boy I was somewhat afraid of the dark when going to bed. I think it was the spooky movies. These scary movies were all the vogue in the 1930's and all the kids went to the movies and got scared to death.

In the 1930's (first half), we always played cowboys and Indians and chased each other all over. Every kid had a cap pistol and the better ones had repeaters with a roll of caps. The fancy automatic pistols cost as much as 25 cents and a roll of caps was 2 cents.

We didn't have television when I was a child. I liked the radio serials such as Jack Armstrong, The All American Boy, H Bar O Ranch cowboy stories and Captain Diamond sea stories. Captain Diamond was a lighthouse keeper, retired from the sea, and he told sea stories. His sponsor was Diamond Crystal Shaker Salt. My family's favorite radio program was Amos and Andy. Jack Armstrong and The Shadow were favorites for Tom and me. Since there was no television, we also played Parcheesi, Chinese checkers, etc., and card games, and jig saw puzzles.

As a child I can remember singing "Old Mac Donald Had a Farm." I also vaguely remember, Tom and me in the bath tub with small boat, etc. I read a series of books in about fourth grade. They were called *Bomba, the Jungle Boy*. I thought they were neat. My favorite book was *Treasure Island* by Robert L. Stevenson.

Ice cream cones in the late 1920's and the 1930's were 5 cents. A big double dip cone was a dime. All loose candy was one cent. Baby Ruths, Hershey Bars, and the like were a nickel. Everybody made chocolate fudge. It was a favorite snack that you made at home. Brownies were not invented yet, at least not in Philadelphia. As I remember, our favorite store when we were kids was Woolworth's Five and Ten Cent Store. Today, kids hang out at the mall.

We never had a swing when I was a kid because there really weren't any trees in our West Philadelphia neighborhood capable of supporting a swing. Nor were there too many tree houses in West Philadelphia. In fact, there were no trees or leaves to burn on Lindenwood Street. There were trees on Yocum Street where my paternal grandparents lived. Leaf burning was a regular event by the adults for the most part. Instead, when we were children, we used to build "bunks" of some sort in back yards or in vacant lots. We built the "bunks" in vacant lots out of 5 gal. cans, wood, stones, etc.

I learned to swim along with all the other kids in the pool at the Kingsessing Recreation Center. We usually went swimming at the public pool or at the New Jersey shore at Wildwood. But, every summer some of the boys went swimming in a swampy lake out along the Pennsylvania Railroad tracks. We hitchhiked with regularity. While in high school and possibly before, we used to hitchhike out Woodland Avenue to Delaware County through Darby, then down U.S. Route Thirteen toward Chester to go swimming in a quarry flooded by rain and springs. It was very clear and deep. My longest hitchhiking trip was from Philadelphia to Washington on a Memorial Day weekend to see the festivities. I did this while I was a cadet on the Schoolship. I saw President Roosevelt at Arlington. Once, three other kids and I walked at least 8 miles round trip to the Philadelphia airport to see the airplanes come in. It turned out to be an all day affair and our parents were wild looking for us.

My father frequently made small toys, etc., for me and he made a stretching frame for drying rabbit and squirrel skins. My father and cousin, Augie Muller were avid small game hunters - ducks, pheasants, rabbits, squirrels, etc. and I went a few times. My mother dutifully cooked up the prizes and we all ate it for dinner. Fred Queroli, Augie Muller and my father used to go rabbit hunting together in Delaware County. My father also went duck hunting in Tinicum near the airport. The double barreled shotgun that belonged to my father was given to him by William Patton (my mother's first cousin, once removed). King, our dog, was an English Setter bird dog, but he was gun shy so he couldn't be used for hunting. The men told my father that King should be shot as he wasn't any good for hunting, but my father wouldn't do it. King stayed at home from then on. He got distemper and had to be put to sleep. I took him to the vet to be "put down" because no one else would do it. He was a big, lovable dog who used to sit on my mother's lap.

As a child, my mother would take us and other kids living on the street on a long walk through the lots and up on the bank overlooking the main line (New York to Washington) of the Pennsylvania Railroad. She had it timed so that in a few minutes the "Congressional Limited" came steaming past at full speed on its way to Washington with my father waving from the locomotive cab. I was a big shot.

When I was in grammar school, a little girl and a little boy died of disease and two boys were killed in accidents. They all lived on or just off 53rd Street. The deaths affected not only me, but most of the other kids also.

I went fishing a few times when I was a kid, but never liked it much. Occasionally, we would catch tadpoles and put them in fish tanks and try to raise frogs. It never worked except for one time. We also used to catch garter snakes (young ones about 10 inches or so). Cartons or bowls were used to hold them. It was a big deal to take them to school in your pocket to scare the girls.

MY TEENAGE YEARS

When Tom and I went to junior high school, my father gave us 25 cents every two weeks when he got paid. The amount increased slowly as we got older. Although we didn't earn our allowance, we worked around the house scrubbing the kitchen floor, vacuuming, etc., but there was seldom any pay involved. My chores as a child were always to scrub the kitchen floor and wash the windows on the outside. We put out trash and ashes (very heavy) when my father wasn't home. We did not have outside chores except cleaning the dog dirt from the backyard. My father did all the painting and washed the car. Tom and I did all the food shopping once we entered junior high school. Before that, shopping was limited to the deli for ham, cheese, Campbell's soup, and the like. My mother bought the major meats - turkey, roast beef, leg of lamb, etc. Shopping was a long walk to the store and loads were heavy.

Traveling carnivals were still the vogue in the 1930's and about three came through every summer and put up tents and stands on a vacant lot for a week or so. There were all the usual rides - ferris wheels, flying swings, crack the whip, merry go rounds, spinning plates, etc. They cost 5 cents and 10 cents a ride. Hot dogs were a nickel.

The strangest thing I ever saw in the sky was a total eclipse of the sun (or nearly so) in Philadelphia about 1934. Everyone was on edge for weeks before the big event.

My favorite time of year when I was a kid was always summer. No school. And maybe January or any time it snowed. Even though summer was my favorite time of year, heat waves were regular every summer in Philadelphia. In row houses with windows only on the front and back and no air-conditioning it was tough to sleep. When we were young, we would get under the hose in the backyard to stay cool. Also, in Philadelphia, the fire hydrant, which was turned on and off all summer, substituted for the suburban sprinkler of later years as a means of keeping cool. As I recall lightning and thunder storms were frequent and severe in Philadelphia in the summer. At least it seems so to me. All the kids ran home in any case.

As a boy, all our vacations were the same, but just what we wanted. My mother, my paternal grandmother, my first cousin Josephine Thompson, Tom, and I went to Wildwood for a month. In fact, we spent most of August through Labor Day at Wildwood in New Jersey. My father and paternal grandfather came down when they could. Also, my mother, Tom, and I went to the Queroli's house in Sea Isle City, New Jersey, for a week or less. As I recall, my father and Fred Queroli came down for a few days.

My mother had a close-knit group of girl friends including Rhoda Berger that she met with once a month until World War II.

When I was a kid, we didn't have best school chums. When we left school for the day we no longer saw our classmates. Our life revolved around the neighborhood especially Lindenwood Street where about 60 children lived. They were your friends and playmates. Very few best chums. Everybody was just called Joe, Marty, Eddie, Frank, and Bill, etc. One kid on our street was called Beezer and the Jewish kid on the next street was called Jewky Greenberg and another was called Bushie Stein. A boy in the next street was named Donald Duckworth. Unfortunately, Walt Disney came out about then with Mickey Mouse and Donald Duck. The poor kid was always known as Donald Duck. We didn't seem to have a best friend in those days. However, I was close to Jim Cosgrove who lived across the street and with Melvin Bee (called Beezer). Incidentally, Beezer was wounded in the Marine Corps and Jim was hurt in a kamikaze attack off the Philippines in World War II. Neither one seriously.

When I was a kid, the usual thing was to buy a kite once. When the paper became torn you re-papered the kite with newspaper or something lighter if you could find it. We all had hundreds of feet of string on a stick. It was a big deal.

Our neighborhood was over 2 miles from the Catholic and the public high schools so no one went out for after school football, etc. The practice fields were even further away. So I did not participate in high school sports. We had local organized and pickup teams and played at a local recreation center called Kingsessing. I played football for the Kingsessing Hawks in 1936. I played tackle and end. We were good.

I could and can still play the harmonica. We had a harmonica band at Sunday School for a couple of years. I was a member of the band. I still have my harmonica (mouth organ) and part of my stamp collection. In fact, my foreign stamp collection was probably my most prized possession when I was young. I was an avid stamp collector as a kid as were many other boys. Procter and Gamble had a weekly radio show where Captain Tim, a world traveler, told worldwide adventure stories about distant lands. You could get all sorts of foreign stamps by sending in Ivory Soap wrappers. We used to go through other people's trash every week looking for Ivory Soap wrappers.

My best talent was probably carpentry and drawing (copying pictures). As an adult, my favorite pastimes include wood working and birding.

MY SCHOOL LIFE

The best advice my mother gave me was to finish high school and stay away from drink.

I went to Benjamin B. Comegys from first to sixth. I attended Anna Howard Shaw junior high school from seventh to ninth and I went to West Philadelphia high school. My first cousin, Josephine Thompson, also graduated from the same three schools, but my brother graduated from John Bartrum high school which opened shortly after I graduated from high school. By the way, Bartrum was located at 70th and Elmwood, if I remember correctly, and we lived at 53rd and Woodland. That was a long walk in those days before there were school buses. Usually we wore a white shirt and knit tie to school and, if classes were cold, we wore a sweater. We wore knickers until sometime in junior high school and then long pants through high school.

The only thing I remember about my first day at school was walking with some other kids about three blocks to Benjamin B. Comegys grammar school. No parents were involved. School was from 8:45 AM to Noon. We walked home for lunch and then had school from 1:20 PM to 3:30 PM. At recess we played running games, tag, etc. There was no playground equipment at the school. Fortunately, my parents never made us wear anything stupid to school except overshoes when it snowed which wasn't very cool.

We walked to and from school, grades one through twelve, rain, shine, or snow, zero degrees to 100 degrees F. It would've been a tough job with my mother to pretend to be sick as an excuse to stay home from school.

OUR PETS

We had lots of pets when we were children, dogs, cats, Guinea pigs, birds, fish, ducks, etc. In fact, my father and all of us tried to raise tropical fish and canaries with a fair degree of success, but the best pet by far was a black-and-white English Setter named King who went everywhere with us and all the gang.

There is a picture of my brother, Tom, with our dog, King, and the Cosgrove's dog taken in 1937 at a swamp called "W" along the railroad tracks in West Philadelphia below 58th and Woodland. King was not a good bird dog so my father did not use him for hunting. King loved my mother and used to sit on her lap.

Tom and King

King

SUMMER CAMP

The only summer camp I had was the Citizens Military Training Camp (CMTC). I was never actually in the armed forces, but Tom and I and other boys from the neighborhood went to the CMTC during summers in high school. The Lindenwood Street gang went together including me, Jim Cosgrove, Larry Caulfield, Moe Goren, Joe Hannan & Ott Reinholt. The purpose of the CMTC was to train us to enter the U.S. Army after we graduated from high school.

First was 30 days infantry training at Fort Meade, Maryland, in 1938 and second was 30 days in field artillery training at Fort Hoyle, Maryland, in 1939. Our parents came down to get us when training was complete.

Fort Meade, Summer 1938

Fort Hoyle, Summer 1939

The minimum age was seventeen years, but many of the boys were sixteen years old and my brother, Tom, got in at fifteen, somehow. Tom served in the Sixth Horse Drawn Field Artillery at Fort Hoyle, Maryland, and in the Third U.S. Cavalry at Fort Belvoir, Virginia. I served in the 34th Infantry at Fort Meade, Maryland, and in the Sixth Field Artillery at Fort Hoyle.

Except at training camp when we slept in tents, we never slept under the stars. It really wasn't done in our area. We tried a few times in the backyard, but mosquitoes were too much. As a kid, we used to build fires in the open field areas, but I never liked roasted hot dogs or marshmallows. I do now.

MY JOBS AS A KID

As a kid, my first job was helper on a laundry truck, picking up and delivering laundry. I also had a newspaper route delivering the afternoon edition of the *Philadelphia Public Ledger*. I gave the route to my first cousin, Skill McCauley, when I was put on the third shift in the tenth grade of high school which didn't let out until 3:45 PM which was too late to walk 3 miles to pick up the papers. The usual pay was about a dollar a day on the laundry truck plus lunch in a diner. Serving newspapers was six days a week plus collecting on Saturday morning. Newspapers were 2 cents each or 12 cents per week. When I collected 12 cents from each customer on Saturday, I got to keep 3 cents, so with 30 customers I usually made 90 cents take home pay.

MY MEDICAL MALADIES

I don't remember ever breaking any bones as a child except that I cracked my nose from football. I never needed any stitches except for the operation on my foot. When I was a child, I had pneumonia, chicken pox, and whopping cough all at the same time. I hardly remember it, but apparently I was very sick. One day when I was little while I was at my Aunt Marge's house, I remember that I got my right ring finger caught in the door. I recall that my mother pulled me in a wagon to 52nd and Chester to visit Dr. Steward. Also, my mother gave us a big bottle of citrate of magnesia every month to clean the poisons out of our body. I had poison ivy many times as a boy. Sometimes all over my body. So did Tom and many other kids.

By far my biggest physical problem was my bad right leg. The foot was limp and the leg was skinny. This was a terrible embarrassment in junior and senior high school. Probably most people never realized it, but I sure did. My right arm was also affected and the lack of power and dexterity in the arm prevented me from playing golf or batting a baseball well. There are three pictures of me taken at the Lulu Temple (pre-Shriners Hospital) which was located on Broad Street. These pictures were taken prior to my operation to lengthen my Achilles tendon. The operation took place in 1926. I was in the Shriners Hospital for seven months on Roosevelt Boulevard in North Philadelphia. I went into the Shriners Hospital at age six. I only had visitors on Sunday and not every week. The worst part was the first ten days when each child was quarantined to prevent the spread of childhood diseases. Even so, I eventually got whopping cough, chicken pox, and pneumonia all at once.

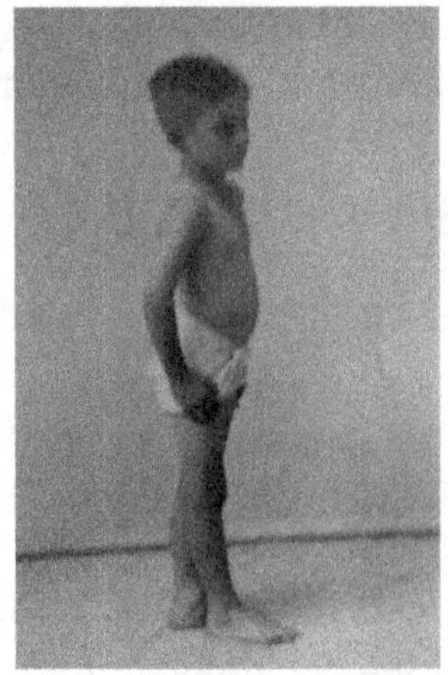
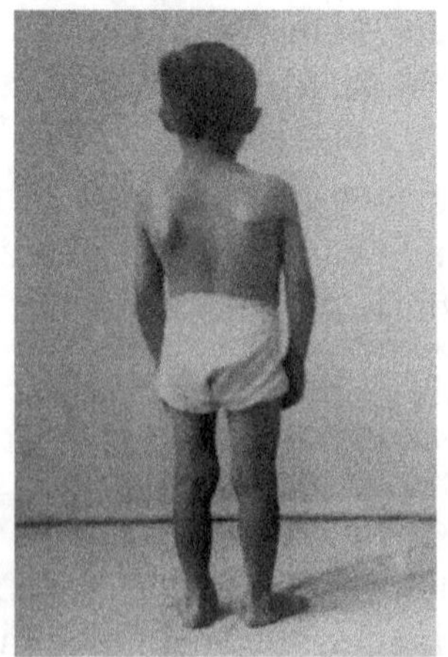
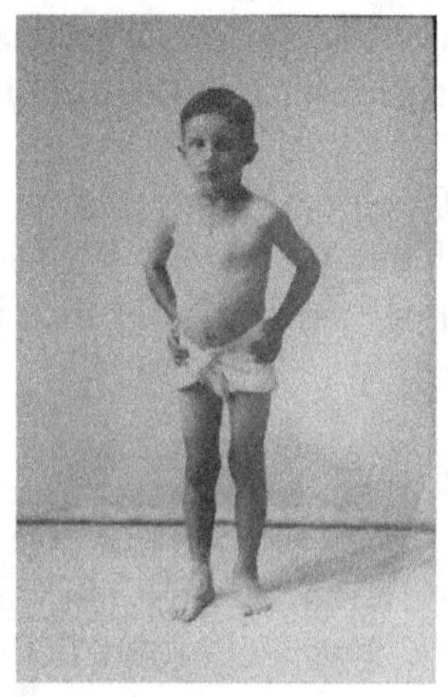

                    Appendix H

BIRTHDAYS, HOLIDAYS, AND SPECIAL EVENTS

Birthdays were not a big event when we lived on Lindenwood Street. My mother always baked a cake and Breyers ice cream was served with the Cosgrove boys across the street sometimes invited. Tom and I always had a homemade cake every year until we left home. I never remember a store bought cake. No party as such. My mother never really made special gifts for us except food and pastries.

I went to Sunday School every Sunday until I was 20. I never missed in sixteen years. I don't know where the medals are now. Although my brother and I were baptized at Tabor Presbyterian Church in South Philadelphia, we attended the First United Presbyterian Church at 52nd and Chester Avenue. My mother made the decision to switch churches when we were old enough to go to Sunday School as the First United Presbyterian Church was within walking distance of our house.

Movies were allowed to open on Sunday in Philadelphia about 1935, but my mother never allowed us to go. We could watch sand lot ball games (baseball and football), but we were not allowed to play. Sunday was not a big day. We were not allowed to swim on Sunday either. Since Tom and I never missed a Sunday in fifteen years, there were not many special memories of going to church. The annual Sunday School picnic was the event of the year. My mother always took the Cosgrove boys from across the street and we had a ball swimming, rock climbing, and all sorts of races plus food. Melvin Bee (Beezer) and I always won the three legged race. The picnics were held at Castle Rock, Pennsylvania or at Glen Rock, New Jersey. Once, Tom and I participated in a Tom Thumb Wedding. The picture is still around here somewhere. He was the best man and I was an usher. It was a full dress affair. The church had occasional covered dish socials, but they were mainly for adults.

Tom Thumb Wedding

Being from the wrong county in Ireland, St. Patrick's Day was not a big event in our lives. Easter, on the other hand, was quite a religious holiday in our house and in our neighborhood. Sunday School and church, of course, and you kept your Sunday best clothes on until late in the day.

May Day was not a big deal on Lindenwood Street. However, it just occurred to me that in the early 1930's when I was in B.B. Comegys School, each class had a May Pole. The girls walked around the pole in opposite directions, weaving in and out, with long multi-colored ribbons.

On Mothers Day, Tom and I wore a red carnation to Sunday School and kept our Sunday clothes on all day.

Memorial Day was usually spent at Mount Moriah Cemetery. All the family went with flowers, etc., to decorate the graves. It was still called Decoration Day by most people. Soldiers fired over the various veterans grave areas. It was a day long affair including walking out and back. When I was in the Boys Brigade, we participated in a big Memorial Day Parade on Broad Street - uniforms, rifles, and all. I remember that one time Tom and I were lined up to go tent camping for two weeks with the Boys Brigade. We were packed and waiting to be picked up on Sunday, but when the station wagon arrived we were told the camp was completely washed out the night before in the rain storm.

On Independence Day, there was the annual parade for kids starting at Comegys School, then Mitchell School, and then Most Blessed Sacrament, and then on to Kingsessing Recreation Center for games and races and free ice cream. Fire crackers were illegal in Philadelphia. They were also illegal with my mother so that was that. Fire crackers were available in Delaware County so there were lots of bangs going off. A big fireworks display was given in Clarks Park at 45th and Kingsessing on the fourth of July night which we all attended. The fourth of July was a big event in the 1930's with parades and fireworks, etc. I think the holidays were used to keep the natives from becoming restless during the Great Depression.

On Halloween, we would dress in a costume and go to all the houses in the neighborhood looking for nuts and fruit. There was no candy given out in those days.

Our only family reunions when I was a child were get-togethers on Thanksgiving and Christmas. Christmas was my favorite holiday - of course. Other holidays were non-events for me for the most part. Our big toy was erector sets and electric trains which were only brought out for a month at Christmas.

When I was young, Thanksgiving was always the same. Roast turkey, stuffing, gravy, homemade cranberry sauce, vegetables, candied sweet potatoes, mashed potatoes, cauliflower au gratin, peas, and creamed onions. We also had homemade pumpkin pie and minced meat pie well laced with whiskey. The guests were usually my paternal grandparents and my first cousin,

Josephine Thompson; Aunt Marge and Uncle John Smith; and sometimes Uncle Willis McCauley and his family including my first cousin Skill McCauley. My mother prepared the dinner which was served only after the Pennsylvania - Cornell football game (on the radio) was finished about 5:00 PM.

I was in several Christmas pageants at Sunday School and church. When I was young, it was the custom to put up the Christmas tree on Christmas Eve day not a week ahead of time as is done today. We decorated the tree with the usual things, balls and tinsel plus an occasional other small ornament. We also hung Christmas stockings. The best Christmas presents we ever received were new units for our large electric train system. My father was a toy train buff. When we were high school age we went to church on Christmas Eve, but not as children. Sometime in the early 1930's, our dog (King) decided to chase the cat who escaped into the living room at full speed and scrambled up the newly trimmed Christmas tree with such vigor that the tree tipped over.

OUR AUTOMOBILES

Our family's first car was a four door 1936 Plymouth. I was fifteen and Tom was thirteen. I don't recall playing any games while riding in the car. In fact, I don't recall any trips except to Delaware County to visit Augie Muller or a very occasional trip to Liberty Grove, Maryland, to visit Uncle John Smith's family.

Our first car cost $700.00 (black). The money came from a $900.00 World War I veterans bonus which was due in 20 years, but Roosevelt had Congress pay it in 1936 to "prime the pump" during the Great Depression. Dad taught me to drive in 1937 when I became sixteen. My mother never learned to drive.

NEW JERSEY

My father was a member of the Masonic Lodge in Camden, New Jersey, not Philadelphia. My father joined the Masons [on March 16, 1943] when they were living on Baird Boulevard in Camden where they moved in the spring of 1942 as far as I can recall. My mother joined the Eastern Star [Camden Chapter 5] about that time [March 7, 1944]. When I returned from my World War II Russian disaster at the end of July 1942, my parents were living in New Jersey.

******

Mary Ann (McCauley) Chambers died on August 8, 1984 at the Masonic Home in Burlington, New Jersey. Henry Grafe Chambers, predeceased her on November 11, 1953. He died suddenly at their home in Collingswood having suffered a major heart attack. They were both buried in the CHAMBERS THOMPSON family plot at Mount Moriah Cemetery in Philadelphia.

Despite his obituary and his widow stating that Henry G. Chambers died the evening of Tuesday, November 10, 1953, his death certificate says he died on November 11, 1953. Mary Ann (McCauley) Chambers always recalled that after she and Harry had eaten dinner together they watched at little television in the livingroom. After they decided to retire for the evening, she suggested that he go ahead and she would follow after tidying up in the kitchen. When she arrived in the bedroom, Mary Ann (McCauley) Chambers said she knew immediately her husband was dead. She called the doctor who came over and pronounced him deceased. The cause of death was a sudden myocardial infarction (heart attack).

The obituary for Henry G. Chambers, always known as Harry, appeared in the *Courier-Post* in Camden, New Jersey, on Wednesday, November 11, 1953. It read as follows:

H. G. Chambers Is Dead at 56

Harry G. Chambers, 56, of 21 Wayne Gardens Apartments, Collingswood, road foreman of engines for the Pennsylvania Reading Seashore Lines, died suddenly Tuesday night at his home.

A native of Philadelphia, Mr. Chambers resided in the Camden area for 13 years. He joined the railroad as a fireman in 1916, was named engineer in 1926, assistant foreman in 1942, and foreman in 1945.

Mr. Chambers was active in Masonic groups. He was a member of Camden Lodge 15, FAM; Tall Cedars of Lebanon, Forest 5; Cyrene Commandery and Siloan Chapter 9, RAM. He was also a member of the Brotherhood of Locomotive Engineers.

Surviving are his widow, Mary two sons, Capt. Thomas W. Chambers, serving with the Army in Korea, and William Scott Chambers, of Havana, Cuba; two grandchildren, and his mother, Mrs. Josephine Chambers, of Philadelphia. Services will be held at 11 a. m. Monday in the Murray Funeral Home, 408 Cooper st., where friends may call Sunday night.

In recalling his father's funeral many years later, William S. Chambers said that it brought back vivid memories of the early 1930s when the railroad brotherhoods were a "big deal" and all his parents' friends worked on the railroad. Even after they moved to Collingswood, all their friends were railroaders. When his father died in South Jersey, there were dozens upon dozens of railroaders at the funeral who arrived from all over including New York, Baltimore, and Washington, D.C., as well as South Jersey and Pennsylvania.

After the death of her husband, Mary Ann (McCauley) Chambers moved back to West Philadelphia where she lived at 1606 S. 53rd Street with her widowed sister, Margaret (McCauley) Smith. When Margaret (McCauley) Smith died in 1957, she left the house at 1606 S. 53rd Street to her sister.

Mary Ann (McCauley) Chambers outlived her husband by 31 years. On March 2, 1972, she sold her home at 1606 S. 53rd Street in West Philadelphia for $8,800.00 and moved to Princeton, New Jersey, to be nearer to her son, William S. Chambers and his family. She lived there in a studio apartment on Palmer Square until she moved to the Masonic Home in Burlington, New Jersey about 1982 where she died suddenly of a myocardial infarction on August 8, 1984, at the age of 92.

Members of the Eastern Star attended her funeral. So did her family all of whom were also present at her burial at Mount Moriah Cemetery where her nephew, David Harrington Marshall, Jr., delivered the committal rite. The obituary of Mary Ann (McCauley) Chambers appeared in the *Philadelphia Inquirer* on Saturday, August 11, 1984. It read as follows:

CHAMBERS

On August 8, 1984, MARYANN wife of the late Henry G. Chambers and mother of the late Thomas W. Chambers at the Masonic Home, Burlington, N.J. She is survived by her son William S. Chambers, 3 granddaughters, Kathryn Torpey, Cynthia S. Chambers and Joann Smith. Funeral services were held Fri. 10:30 A.M at the Masonic Home Chapel, Burlington, N. J. Int. was in Mt. Moriah Cem, Phila.

Wallace Families in Mullaghinch
Aghadowey Parish, County Londonderry, Ireland

The following two reports with accompanying map were written by George Gilmore, geo.gil@hotmail.co.uk, who was born and grew up near Aghadowey Presbyterian Church. He recorded all the headstones in the cemetery in the early 1980s. He also looked after the plots, the burials, as well as the installation and maintenance of the headstones for many years while he was on the graveyard committee.

The two reports and the map include information about the occupants of three farms in Mullaghinch at the time of the Ironmongers Company (i.e, the landlord's) visitation that took place in 1863. The conclusions reached by George Gilmore concerning members of the McCauley, Patton, and Wallace families that migrated to Philadelphia are as follows:

FARM 15: Stephen Wallace who married Letitia Gormley at Tabor Presbyterian Church in Philadelphia in 1852 is believed to be the son of William and Mary Ann Wallace who occupied Farm 15. Mary Ann Wallace died in 1852. She is buried in the Aghadowey Presbyterian Graveyard. Her headstone reads as follows:

Plot 201 Aghadowey Presbyterian Graveyard
Stephen Wallace of Charlestown S.C. To the memory of his mother
Mary Ann Wallace late of Mullahinch who departed this life
April 10th 1852 aged 61 years

Note: Plot 201 where Stephen Wallace erected the headstone to his mother, Mary Ann Wallace, is next to Plot 202, which is unmarked, but in the name of Samuel Wallace of Farm 16. This arrangement usually means there is a close family connection between the two families.

FARM 16: Margaret Wallace who married Stephen McCauley at Aghadowey Presbyterian Church in Mullaghinch in 1848 and her sister, Nancy Wallace, who marred William Patton in 1860 at Westminster Presbyterian Church in Philadelphia are believed to be the daughters of Thomas and Isabella Wallace who occupied Farm 16. Thomas and Isabella Wallace died in 1853 and 1868, respectively, and are buried in the Aghadowey Presbyterian Graveyard. Their headstone reads as follows:

Plot 295 Aghadowey Presbyterian Graveyard
Erected by John Wallace of Mullahinch to the memory of his father
Thomas Wallace who died 7th July 1853 aged 75 years. Also his mother
Isabella Wallace who died 10th October 1868 aged 74 years. And
his beloved wife Margaret Ann Wallace who died 21st August 1880 aged 50 years.

FARM 17: Stephen Wallace who married Letitia Gormley at Tabor Presbyterian Church in Philadelphia in 1852 is also believed to be the nephew of Stephen Wallace. That is, William Wallace of Farm 15 and Stephen Wallace of Farm 17 are believed to have been brothers.

Map of Mullaghinch, Aghadowey Parish, County Londonderry, Ireland

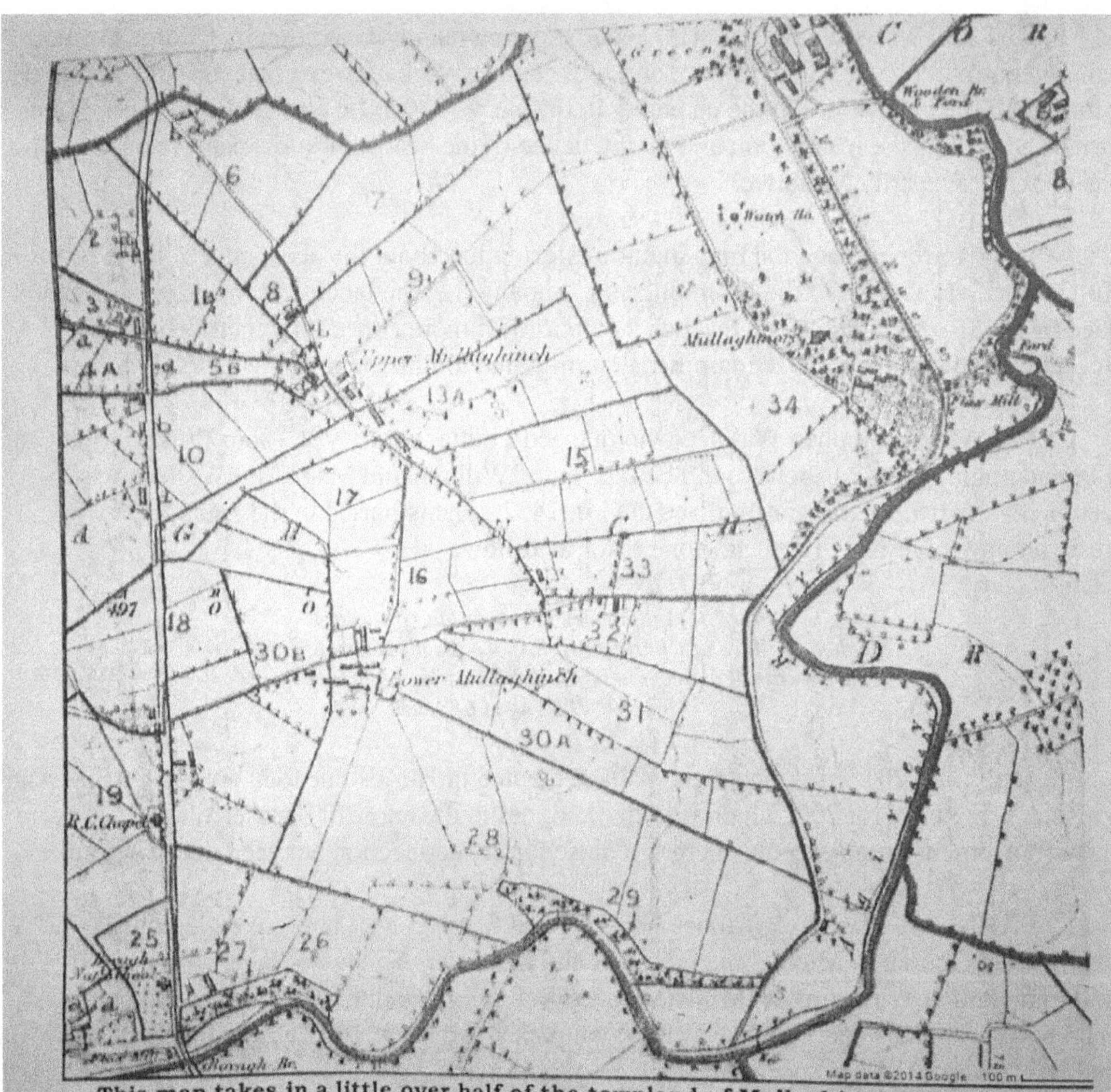

This map takes in a little over half of the townland of Mullaghinch/Mullahinch. Total area is 496 acres 2roods 37 perches, not a lot if you consider a square mile is 640 acres. This is the valuation map for c1860, each farm is identified with a number. I am also adding notes from a visitation by the Ironmongers Co. in 1863.

15 William Wallace 12a 1r 20p *"Wife, three children. The women pleads hard for a fireplace in her bedroom. Asks for a few bricks, which we promised."*

16 John Wallace 9a 1r 15p *"John Wallace jun. Mother (blind) and sister. A very poor cottage."*

17 Stephen Wallace 4a 1r 0p. Changed to John Wallace sen c1862. *"Wife, four children. Not very tidy."*

Report 1
WALLACE FAMILIES (1) MULLAHINCH

FARM 15. WILLIAM WALLACE 12A 2R 30P

Marriage Coleraine Registry Office 19th Nov 1856
William Wallace farmer Mullahinch son of William Wallace farmer to
Rachel Beers widow Killykergan daughter of James Steen engineman

Marriage Main Street (2nd) Garvagh Presbyterian Church 24th Feb 1853
Thomas Wallace farmer Mullahinch son of Robert Wallace farmer to
Elizabeth Wallace Mullahinch daughter of William Wallace farmer

Marriage Aghadowey Presbyterian Church 26th May 1886
William Wallace farmer Mullahinch son of William Wallace farmer to
Margaret Anne Wallace Mullahinch daughter of John Wallace farmer

Plot 217 Aghadowey Presbyterian Graveyard
In loving memory of Bessie beloved wife of John Wallace who died
10th July 1894 aged 70 years. The above named John Wallace who
died March 1898. Their daughter Maggie who died 8th April 1922.
Their son William who died 4th Oct 1932. Also their grandchildren
Bessie Knox died 19th March 1952. Stephen died in New Zealand
18th June 1956. John died 30th August 1972. William died
28th December 1973. Martha Jane died 7th October 1979.
Erected by their son William & Stephen of California.

Plot 201 Aghadowey Presbyterian Graveyard
Stephen Wallace of Charlestown S.C. To the memory of his mother
Mary Ann Wallace late of Mullahinch who departed this life
April 10th 1852 aged 61 years

Joseph Wallace lived in a house with small garden on William's property
until c1885 (valuation revisions). The death indexes show that Joseph Wallace
born 1804 died Oct/Dec 1884 who may be the same person.

This is where the last Wallace's lived in Mullahinch until the 1970's and
the Knox family acquired the land 15, 16 & 17. William Knox b. 1953
got married in 1982 and renovated the old Wallace homestead near the
Knox farmhouse and has been living in it since.

WILLS:
John Wallace sen Mullahinch farmer died 28th March 1898

Margaret Wallace Mullahinch married women died 8th April 1922
William Wallace Mullahinch farmer died 27th Jan 1929.

FARM 16. JOHN WALLACE 9A 1R 15P

Marriage Aghadowey Presbyterian Church 8th Nov 1859
Robert Wallace farmer Claggin son of Thomas Wallace farmer to
Anne McIlroy Mullamore daughter of Robert McIlroy farmer

Marriage Moneydig Presbyterian Church 6th June 1865
John Wallace farmer Mullahinch son of Thos. Wallace farmer to
Margaret Ann Boyd Drumeen daughter of John Boyd farmer

Marriage Aghadowey Presbyterian Church 1st Sept 1865
John Wallace labourer Mullahinch son of John Wallace labourer to
Isabella Wallace Mullahinch daughter of Thomas Wallace farmer

Marriage Macosquin Presbyterian Church 20th July 1882
John Wallace (wid) farmer Mullahinch son of Thomas Wallace
farmer to Mary Jamieson Managher daughter of Robert Jamieson farmer

Plot 188 Aghadowey Presbyterian Graveyard
In Memorian John Wallace Halftown Mullahinch died June 1880
aged 30 years. Isabella his beloved wife died 1894 aged 50 years.

Plot 295 Aghadowey Presbyterian Graveyard
Erected by John Wallace of Mullahinch to the memory of his father
Thomas Wallace who died 7th July 1853 aged 75 years. Also his mother
Isabella Wallace who died 10th October 1868 aged 74 years. And
his beloved wife Margaret Ann Wallace who died 21st August 1880 aged 50 years.

The valuation revisions show that this farm (No 16) was taken over
by William Wallace (No 15) c1903. The dwelling house was down by 1914

WILLS:
Isabella Wallace Mullahinch died 14th June 1894 mentions
her sister-in-law Betty McIntyre and her brother John Wallace Mullahinch
Robert Wallace Claggan died 14th March 1892 sons John, William,
Robert and James, daughters Jane McIlroy and Margaret
NOTE: 1863 tenants notes Mullahinch Robert Wallace 7a 1r 30p (land only)
"See also Claggan"

FARM 17. STEPHEN WALLACE 4A 1R 0P

Marriage Aghadowey Presbyterian Church 4th Feb 1848
John Wallace farmer Mullahinch son of Stephen Wallace farmer to
Bessie Knox Mullahinch daughter of Samuel Knox farmer

Marriage Aghadowey Presbyterian Church 28th April 1848
Samuel Querns? Cornamucklagh son of Denis Querns? weaver to
Mace Jane Wallace Mullahinch daughter of Stephen Wallace farmer

Marriage Aghadowey Presbyterian Church 30th Dec 1881
John Cochrane 20 farmer Mullahinch son of John Cochrane farmer to
Martha Jane Wallace 19 Mullahinch daughter of John Wallace farmer

Baptisms Aghadowey Presbyterian Church
Margaret Wallace daughter of John Mullahinch baptised 7th June 1857
Nancy Wallace daughter of John Mullahinch baptised 17th Nov 1858
Martha Jane Wallace daughter Mullahinch baptised 2nd Sept 1860

Plot 217 Aghadowey Presbyterian Graveyard
In loving memory of Bessie beloved wife of John Wallace who died
10th July 1894 aged 70 years. The above named John Wallace who
died March 1898. Their daughter Maggie who died 8th April 1922.
Their son William who died 4th Oct 1932. Also their grandchildren
Bessie Knox died 19th March 1952. Stephen died in New Zealand
18th June 1956. John died 30th August 1972. William died
28th December 1973. Martha Jane died 7th October 1979.
Erected by their son William & Stephen of California.

The valuation revisions show that this farm (No 17) was taken over by
William Wallace (No 15) c1902. By 1914 the dwelling house was in
poor condition and in 1922 a ruin.

The Wallace's that died in the 1970's were the last to live in Mullahinch

****

Marriage Main Street (2nd) Garvagh Presbyterian Church 9th July 1853
William Wallace bleacher Mullahinch son of John Wallace bleacher to
Martha Knox Mullahinch daughter of James Knox labourer

Marriage Main Street (2nd) Garvagh Presbyterian Church 6th January 1854
George McCauley labourer Gortan son of Alex McCauley bleacher to

Jane Wallace Mullahinch daughter of John Wallace farmer

Marriage Coleraine Registry Office 2nd August 1856
William McAteer labourer Bovagh son of Thomas McAteer labourer to
*Elizabeth Wallace Mullahinch daughter of John Wallace farmer

Marriage Main Street (2nd) Garvagh Presbyterian Church 21st May 1857
James Wallace bleacher Mullahinch son of John Wallace weaver to
Mary Neily Drumeal Aghadowey daughter of James Neily farmer

Marriage Aghadowey Presbyterian Church 1st September 1865
*John Wallace labourer Mullahinch son of John Wallace labourer to
Isabella Wallace Mullahinch daughter of Thomas Wallace farmer

William McAteer (sic) who married Elizabeth Wallace in 1856 was
really William McIntyre so when Isabella Wallace in her Will dated
13th June 1894 left £10 to her sister-in-law Betty McIntyre; this means
Elizabeth/Betty was a sister of Isabella's husband John. The age I have
for John on the headstone can't be right as he would have been 15 when
he was married.

When William Wallace who married Martha Knox 1853 applied for
the pension which had just become available in 1908, the 1841 and
1851 census records were used to check the applicant's age. This
was before these census records were destroyed and the results of a
lot of these checks survive. William was eleven in 1841at Mullahinch
and when he died at Ballygawley 22nd February 1917 his age was 87
which in both cases result in a birth date of 1830. William's mother's
name was given as Sarah Wallace.

WALLACE FAMILIES (2) MULLAGHINCH

Mullaghinch with the 'g' seems to be the officially correct spelling but it is more often found without the 'g'.

In the1831 (census) there are the following seven Wallace households in Mullahinch and two years later the tithe books show who had land.

5 Wm. Wallace	4 male 2 female		10 acres		13a 2r 9p in 1842 15?
42 John Wallace	1	1			
44 Robt. Wallace	3	5		8 acres	11a 1r 33p in 1842
45 Widw. Wallace	3	3			
50 Thomas Wallace	2	2		5 acres jun.	7a 0r 38p in 1842 16?
52 Thos. Wallace	3	5	sen.	7 acres	8a 2r 14p in 1842 16?
53 Stephen Wallace	5	4		3 acres	4a 0r 25p in 1842 17

In Nolan's 1842 survey there is a Widow Wallace and William Wallace holding 13 acres 2 roods 9 perches which may be the same as the following:

FARM 15 - WILLIAM WALLACE

William Wallace married Mary Ann born c 1791 died 1852 and was succeeded in farm (15) by his son William Wallace

1.   William Wallace born unknown died unknown married in Coleraine Registry Office 19th November 1856 Rachel Beers widow Killykergan, daughter of James Steen engineman. According to the tenants notes 1863 they had three (sic) children

   A.   William Wallace born c1857 died 27th January 1929 married in Aghadowey Presbyterian Church 26th May 1886 Margaret Ann Wallace daughter of John Wallace farmer Mullahinch.
      a.   Stephen Wallace born 1887 emigrated to New Zealand a few years before W.W.1 and joined the New Zealand Expeditionary Force, survived the war and died in New Zealand 18th June 1956
      b.   William Wallace born 1889 died 28th December 1973
      c.   Bessie Knox Wallace born 17th July 1891 died 19th March 1952
      d.   John Wallace born 30th November 1893 died 30th August 1972 unmarried
      e.   Martha Jane Wallace born 1897 died 7th October 1979 unmarried

2.   Elizabeth Wallace married in Main Street Presbyterian Church Garvagh 24th February 1853 Thomas Wallace farmer Mullahinch son of Robert Wallace farmer

3.   **Stephen Wallace born c 1829 died unknown married in Philadelphia 1852 Letitia Gormley 1827-1914**

NOTE: I believe this to be Stephen Wallace's family and Stephen Wallace in farm (17) his uncle. I also believe that Thomas Wallace in farm (16) is closely connected.

FARM 16 - THOMAS WALLACE

Thomas Wallace born c 1778 died 7th July 1853 and his wife Isabella born c1794 died 10th October 1868. Thomas Wallace was succeeded in the farm (16) by his son John Wallace.

1.   Robert Wallace born c 1813 died 14th March 1892 married in Aghadowey Presbyterian Church 8th November 1859 Anne McIlroy daughter of Robert McIlroy farmer Mullamore. Robert had land at Mullahinch but lived at Clagan

2.   **Margaret Wallace born 1823 died Philadelphia 3rd January 1860 married in Aghadowey Presbyterian Church 11th July 1848 Stephen McAuley farmer Mullahinch born May 1817 died 2nd August 1903 Philadelphia son of Neal McAuley farmer**

3.   John Wallace born c 1826 died after 1901 married in Moneydig Presbyterian Church 6th June 1865 Margaret Ann Boyd b c 1830 died 21st August 1880 daughter of John Boyd farmer Drumeen. John married a second time in Macosquin Presbyterian Church 20th July 1882 Mary Jamieson b c 1836 daughter of Robert Jamieson farmer Managher

4.   Isabella Wallace born c 1838 died 14th June 1894 married in Aghadowey Presbyterian Church 1st September 1865 John Wallace labourer Mullahinch son of John Wallace labourer. Lived at the "Halftown" Mullahinch. In her Will she mentions her sister-in-law Betty McIntyre and her brother John Wallace Mullahinch and also "I direct that my dwelling house with garden and premises thereto attached and turf bank and which I have bought out from the Ironmongers Company with my own money shall be sold." See NOTE below.

5.   **Nancy Wallace younger sister of Margaret McAuley also emigrated to U.S.**

NOTE: Various records between the 1830's and the 1850's show that there was a Thomas Wallace senr and Thomas junr. In the Aghadowey Church stipend lists Thomas senr and Thomas junr sat in the same pew number 77. It is not clear if the above are all the one family. Robert may not be.

In Griffiths valuation c1859 a Jane Wallace was living in a house with a garden (20c) on John Cochrane's farm. In 1863 it was noted she was "A poor old woman" although she lived there for another twenty years or so. This appears to be the same house that Isabella bought from the Ironmongers Company (landlords) just a few years before she died.

Samuel Wallace had 15a 1r 20p (at the "Halftown" Mullahinch) in 1863 when it was noted he had three sisters and one nephew. He probably died around 1877-78 as the farm was in John McAlister's name in 1879.

Plot 202 in Aghadowey Presbyterian Graveyard although unmarked is in the name of Samuel Wallace and is next to the plot where Stephen Wallace erected the headstone which usually means a close family connection.

FARM 17 - STEPHEN WALLACE

Stephen Wallace probably died c 1862 and was succeeded in the farm (17) by his son John.

1.   John Wallace born 1824 died 28th March 1898, married in Aghadowey Presbyterian Church 4th February 1848 Bessie Knox born 1824 died 10th July 1894 daughter of Samuel Knox farmer Mullahinch and had family:

    A.   William Wallace born 7th March 1851 died 4th October 1932

    B.   Margaret Anne (Maggie) Wallace baptised 7th June 1857 died 8th April 1922, married in Aghadowey Presbyterian Church 26th May 1886 William Wallace farmer Mullahinch born c1857 died 27th January 1929 son of William Wallace farmer

        a.   Stephen Wallace born 1887 died in New Zealand 18th June 1956

        b.   William Wallace born 1889 died 28th December 1973

        c.   Bessie Knox Wallace born 17th July 1891 died

        d.   John Wallace born 30th November 1893 died 30th August 1972 unmarried

        e.   Martha Jane Wallace born 1897 died 7th October 1979 unmarried

    C.   Nancy Wallace baptized 17th November 1858

    D.   Martha Jane Wallace baptized 2nd September 1860 died 29th December 1947, married in Aghadowey Presbyterian Church 30th December 1881 John Cochrane farmer Mullahinch born c1852 died 3rd May 1927 son of John Cochrane farmer

        a.   John Cochrane born 7th October 1882 died 27th April 1970 Silver Bow Co., Montana, departed Londonderry for New York on the "City of Rome 15th June 1901 with his sister Bessie and uncle William Wallace. John married at Silver Bow Co., 21st November 1907 Winnefred Jane Tretheway 1882-1943

        b.   Bessie Cochrane born 29th September 1884 died 28th September 1966 Maryland, emigrated with her brother John 1901, married at Bute City (Silver Bow Co.) Montana 22nd November 1905 Edward Owen Roberts

        c.   William Cochrane born c1887 died 2nd July 1976 married in Aghadowey

Presbyterian Church 19th October 1921 Kathleen Hull teacher Segorry daughter of Wm. Hull farmer

d. Sarah Cochrane born 17th July 1889 died 1st June 1974 Rosetown Saskatchewan, boarded the "Caronia" at Liverpool for Halifax Nova Scotia 21st June 1920 (teacher) "to marry a farmer"

e. Maggie Cochrane born 22nd October 1891 died Married in Aghadowey Presbyterian Church 26th December 1918 John Burnside farmer Edenbane son of James Burnside farmer

f. Robert Cochrane born 15th July 1894? died at the Royal Victoria Hospital, Belfast, 11th September 1962

g. Stephen Wallace Cochrane born 7th February 1896 died 9th November 1981Saskatchewan, emigrated with his sister Sarah in 1920, married in Granshaw Presbyterian Church, Comber 19th February 1930 Edith S. Browne daughter of Samuel Browne Lisleen Comber Co Down

h. Martha Jane Cochrane born 7th May 1899 died 27th May 1899

2. Mace Jane Wallace born unknown died unknown married in Aghadowey Presbyterian Church 28th April 1848 Samuel Querns Cornamucklagh son of Denis Querns weaver

Descendants of Stephen McCauley

Generation 1

1. **STEPHEN[1] MCCAULEY** was born in May 1817 in Mullaghinch, Aghadowey Parish, County Londonderry, Ireland. He died on 02 Aug 1903 in Philadelphia, Pennsylvania. He married Margaret Wallace, daughter of Thomas Wallace and Isabella on 11 Jul 1848 in Aghadowey, Aghadowey Parish, Co. Londonderry, Ireland. She was born about 1823 in Mullaghinch, Aghadowey Parish, County Londonderry, Ireland. She died on 03 Jan 1860 in Philadelphia, Pennsylvania.

Stephen McCauley and Margaret Wallace had the following children:

    i.   JAMES[2] MCCAULEY was born in 1849 in Mullaghinch, Aghadowey Parish, County Londonderry, Ireland. He died on 04 Jun 1889 in Philadelphia, Pennsylvania.

2.   ii.   THOMAS MCCAULEY was born on 14 Feb 1854 in Philadelphia, Pennsylvania. He died on 08 Aug 1925 in Philadelphia, Pennsylvania. He married Mary Ann Wallace, daughter of Stephen Wallace and Letitia Montgomery Gormley on 20 Nov 1879 in Philadelphia, Pennsylvania. She was born on 25 Nov 1854 in Charleston, Charleston County, South Carolina. She died on 31 Dec 1909 in Philadelphia, Pennsylvania.

3.   iii.   MARGARET MCCAULEY was born on 10 Dec 1856 in Philadelphia, Pennsylvania. She died on 04 Nov 1939 in Norwood, Delaware County, Pennsylvania. She married Robert Wright, son of Hugh Wright and Margaret McCorkle on 27 Apr 1885 in Philadelphia, Pennsylvania. He was born on 24 Oct 1864 in Londonderry, Ireland. He died on 11 Jan 1908 in Philadelphia, Pennsylvania.

Generation 2

2. **THOMAS[2] MCCAULEY** (Stephen[1]) was born on 14 Feb 1854 in Philadelphia, Pennsylvania. He died on 08 Aug 1925 in Philadelphia, Pennsylvania. He married Mary Ann Wallace, daughter of Stephen Wallace and Letitia Montgomery Gormley on 20 Nov 1879 in Philadelphia, Pennsylvania. She was born on 25 Nov 1854 in Charleston, Charleston County, South Carolina. She died on 31 Dec 1909 in Philadelphia, Pennsylvania.

Thomas McCauley and Mary Ann Wallace had the following children:

    i.   LETITIA[3] MCCAULEY was born on 06 Dec 1880 in Philadelphia, Pennsylvania. She died on 01 Jan 1883 in Philadelphia, Pennsylvania.

    ii.   MARGARET MCCAULEY was born on 10 Oct 1883 in Philadelphia, Pennsylvania. She died on 01 May 1957 in Philadelphia, Pennsylvania. She married John Thomas Smith, son of John T. Smith and Sarah McNutt on 24 Oct 1925 in Philadelphia, Pennsylvania. He was born on 03 Mar 1872 in Harford County, Maryland. He died on 24 Feb 1949 in Philadelphia, Pennsylvania.

    iii.   LETITIA WALLACE MCCAULEY was born on 26 Jul 1885 in Philadelphia, Pennsylvania. She died on 30 Jan 1908 in Philadelphia, Pennsylvania.

    iv.   THOMAS WALLACE MCCAULEY was born in Oct 1888 in Philadelphia, Pennsylvania. He died on 05 Apr 1890 in Philadelphia, Pennsylvania.

4.   v.   MARY ANN MCCAULEY was born on 07 Jul 1892 in Philadelphia, Pennsylvania. She died on 08 Aug 1984 in Burlington Township, Burlington County, New Jersey. She married Henry Grafe Chambers, son of William Scott Chambers and Josephine

Irene Reitze on 30 Jul 1918 in Philadelphia, Pennsylvania. He was born on 08 Jan 1897 in Philadelphia, Pennsylvania. He died on 11 Nov 1953 in Collingswood, Camden County, New Jersey.

5.   vi.   WILLIS SKILLMAN MCCAULEY SR. was born on 08 Sep 1896 in Philadelphia, Pennsylvania. He died on 10 Sep 1970 in Philadelphia, Pennsylvania. He married Mae Schwartz, daughter of John Schwartz and Mary on 30 Jan 1921 in Elkton, Maryland. She was born on 18 Feb 1894 in Philadelphia, Pennsylvania. She died on 28 Jun 1982 in Philadelphia, Pennsylvania.

3.   MARGARET[2] MCCAULEY (Stephen[1]) was born on 10 Dec 1856 in Philadelphia, Pennsylvania. She died on 04 Nov 1939 in Norwood, Delaware County, Pennsylvania. She married Robert Wright, son of Hugh Wright and Margaret McCorkle on 27 Apr 1885 in Philadelphia, Pennsylvania. He was born on 24 Oct 1864 in Londonderry, Ireland. He died on 11 Jan 1908 in Philadelphia, Pennsylvania.

Robert Wright and Margaret McCauley had the following children:

    i.   ROBERT[3] WRIGHT JR. was born on 13 Jan 1888 in Philadelphia, Pennsylvania. He died on 13 Feb 1893 in Philadelphia, Pennsylvania.

    ii.   THOMAS WALLACE WRIGHT was born on 10 Apr 1890 in Philadelphia, Pennsylvania. He died on 12 Feb 1891 in Philadelphia, Pennsylvania.

6.   iii.   MARGARET ANN WRIGHT was born on 31 Dec 1891 in Philadelphia, Pennsylvania. She died on 01 Feb 1974 in Glenolden, Delaware County, Pennsylvania. She married August C. Muller, son of Frederick W. Muller Sr. and Margaret Reedy on 28 May 1917 in Philadelphia, Pennsylvania. He was born on 22 Sep 1888 in Philadelphia, Pennsylvania. He died on 14 Jan 1951 in Norwood, Delaware County, Pennsylvania.

7.   iv.   AGNES WALLACE WRIGHT was born on 14 Nov 1893 in Philadelphia, Pennsylvania. She died on 21 Nov 1934 in Wynnewood, Montgomery County, Pennsylvania, USA. She married Earl Seitzinger Berger Sr., son of Albert Berger and Emma Seitzinger on 07 Feb 1913 in Wilmington, New Castle County, Delaware. He was born on 05 Nov 1891 in Strawberry Mansion, Philadelphia, Pennsylvania. He died on 23 Jan 1967 in Reading, Pennsylvania.

Generation 3

4.   MARY ANN[3] MCCAULEY (Thomas[2], Stephen[1]) was born on 07 Jul 1892 in Philadelphia, Pennsylvania. She died on 08 Aug 1984 in Burlington Township, Burlington County, New Jersey. She married Henry Grafe Chambers, son of William Scott Chambers and Josephine Irene Reitze on 30 Jul 1918 in Philadelphia, Pennsylvania. He was born on 08 Jan 1897 in Philadelphia, Pennsylvania. He died on 11 Nov 1953 in Collingswood, Camden County, New Jersey.

Henry Grafe Chambers and Mary Ann McCauley had the following children:

    i.   WILLIAM SCOTT[4] CHAMBERS was born on 25 Feb 1921 in Philadelphia, Pennsylvania. He died on 08 Feb 2014 in Plantation Broward County Florida. He married Gloria Ann Freda, daughter of Guerino Angelo Maria Freda and Filomena M. Quaresima on 26 Jan 1946 in Princeton, Mercer County, New Jersey. She was born on 06 Mar 1921 in Princeton, Mercer County, New Jersey. She died on 28 Aug 1987 in Portsmouth, Virginia.

ii. THOMAS WALLACE CHAMBERS was born on 25 Mar 1923 in Philadelphia, Pennsylvania. He died on 06 Oct 1955 in Stateburg, Sumter County, South Carolina. He married Florence Clark, daughter of James Freeman Clark and Anna Lee on 31 May 1948 in New Castle, New Castle County, Delaware. She was born on 13 Apr 1930 in Haddonfield, Camden County, New Jersey. She died on 16 Feb 2016 in Churchville, Bucks County, Pennsylvania.

5. WILLIS SKILLMAN[3] MCCAULEY SR. (Thomas[2], Stephen[1]) was born on 08 Sep 1896 in Philadelphia, Pennsylvania. He died on 10 Sep 1970 in Philadelphia, Pennsylvania. He married Mae Schwartz, daughter of John Schwartz and Mary on 30 Jan 1921 in Elkton, Maryland. She was born on 18 Feb 1894 in Philadelphia, Pennsylvania. She died on 28 Jun 1982 in Philadelphia, Pennsylvania.

Willis Skillman McCauley Sr. and Mae Schwartz had the following child:
   i. WILLIS SKILLMAN[4] MCCAULEY JR. was born on 13 Jan 1922 in Philadelphia, Pennsylvania. He died on 04 Nov 2002 in Harleysville, Montgomery County, Pennsylvania.

6. MARGARET ANN[3] WRIGHT (Margaret[2] McCauley, Stephen[1] McCauley) was born on 31 Dec 1891 in Philadelphia, Pennsylvania. She died on 01 Feb 1974 in Glenolden, Delaware County, Pennsylvania. She married August C. Muller, son of Frederick W. Muller Sr. and Margaret Reedy on 28 May 1917 in Philadelphia, Pennsylvania. He was born on 22 Sep 1888 in Philadelphia, Pennsylvania. He died on 14 Jan 1951 in Norwood, Delaware County, Pennsylvania.

August C. Muller and Margaret Ann Wright had the following children:
   i. VIRGINIA LORRAINE[4] MULLER was born on 16 Nov 1919 in Philadelphia, Pennsylvania. She died on 24 Sep 1993 in Bristol, Bucks County, Pennsylvania. She married Robert Randolph Figart on 16 Apr 1949 in Sharon Hill, Pennsylvania. He was born on 10 Apr 1913 in Altoona, Blair County, Pennsylvania. He died on 14 Oct 1975 in Levittown, Bucks County, Pennsylvania.

   ii. MARION ELAINE MULLER was born on 20 Aug 1927 in Orvilla, Montgomery County, Pennsylvania. She died on 28 Sep 2006 in Fountain Lake, Garland County, Arkansas. She married Edgar D. Wilson on 15 Oct 1960 in Norwood, Delaware County, Pennsylvania. He was born on 10 Aug 1932 in Dumbarton, Scotland.

7. AGNES WALLACE[3] WRIGHT (Margaret[2] McCauley, Stephen[1] McCauley) was born on 14 Nov 1893 in Philadelphia, Pennsylvania. She died on 21 Nov 1934 in Wynnewood, Montgomery County, Pennsylvania, USA. She married Earl Seitzinger Berger Sr., son of Albert Berger and Emma Seitzinger on 07 Feb 1913 in Wilmington, New Castle County, Delaware. He was born on 05 Nov 1891 in Strawberry Mansion, Philadelphia, Pennsylvania. He died on 23 Jan 1967 in Reading, Pennsylvania.

Earl Seitzinger Berger Sr. and Agnes Wallace Wright had the following children:
   i. EARL SEITZINGER[4] BERGER JR. was born on 27 Oct 1913 in Philadelphia, Pennsylvania. He died on 29 Aug 1941 in Philadelphia, Philadelphia.

   ii. EMMA WRIGHT BERGER was born on 21 May 1915 in Philadelphia, Pennsylvania. She died on 07 May 1999 in Upper Darby, Delaware County, Pennsylvania.

   iii. MARGARET WALLACE BERGER was born on 10 Dec 1917 in Philadelphia,

Pennsylvania. She died on 21 Aug 1995 in Bywood, Upper Darby, Delaware County, Pennsylvania. She married Harry Edward Filler, son of Edward Filler and Edna Evans on 22 Nov 1950 in Arlington County, Virginia. He was born on 09 May 1909. He died on 06 Mar 1984.

iv. ROBERT BERGER was born on 09 Jun 1920 in Philadelphia, Pennsylvania. He died on 25 Dec 1944 in Cherbourg, France (World War II). He married Eleanor Anderson, daughter of Robert Anderson and Ella McCarthy on 18 Aug 1944 in Pittsburgh, Allegheny, Pennsylvania. She was born on 10 Jun 1923 in Pittsburgh, Allegheny County, Pennsylvania. She died on 21 Oct 2012 in Orange, Orange County, Texas.

Kinship Report for Stephen McCauley

Name:	Birth Date:	Relationship:
Anderson, Eleanor	10 Jun 1923	Wife of great grandson
Baker, Dylan Bruce	31 Mar 2016	4th great grandson
Baker, Jeffrey Paul	01 Nov 1982	Husband of 3rd great granddaughter
Benjamin, Haim	21 May 1986	Husband of 3rd great granddaughter
Benjamin, Jacob Isaac	22 Dec 2018	4th great grandson
Berger, Earl Seitzinger Sr.	05 Nov 1891	Husband of granddaughter
Berger, Earl Seitzinger Jr.	27 Oct 1913	Great grandson
Berger, Emma Wright	21 May 1915	Great granddaughter
Berger, Margaret Wallace	10 Dec 1917	Great granddaughter
Berger, Robert	09 Jun 1920	Great grandson
Chambers, Cynthia Scott	05 Mar 1953	2nd great granddaughter
Chambers, Henry Grafe	08 Jan 1897	Husband of granddaughter
Chambers, Jo-Ann	05 Jul 1955	2nd great granddaughter
Chambers, Kathryn Judith	26 Mar 1947	2nd great granddaughter
Chambers, Thomas Wallace	25 Mar 1923	Great grandson
Chambers, William Scott	25 Feb 1921	Great grandson
Clark, Florence	13 Apr 1930	Wife of great grandson
Elchert, Abigail		4th great granddaughter
Elchert, Anthony Giovanni	16 Jan 2004	4th great grandson
Elchert, Eugene Francis	03 Apr 1979	Husband of 3rd great granddaughter
Elchert, Lynn Marie Elchert	14 Jan 2005	4th great granddaughter
Figart, Charlotte	07 Mar 1994	3rd great granddaughter
Figart, David Randolph	31 Oct 1958	2nd great grandson
Figart, David Randolph II	24 Jun 1998	3rd great grandson
Figart, Emily	17 Feb 1993	3rd great granddaughter
Figart, Kay Lorraine	24 Sep 1984	3rd great granddaughter
Figart, Robert Randolph	10 Apr 1913	Husband of great granddaughter
Figart, Roberta Lynn	08 Jul 1953	2nd great granddaughter
Filler, Christy	Abt. 1976	3rd great granddaughter
Filler, Harry Edward	09 May 1909	Husband of great granddaughter
Filler, Harry Edward	05 Dec 1942	2nd great grandson
Filler, Janet	1948	2nd great granddaughter
Filler, Robert Earl	23 Feb 1946	2nd great grandson
Filler, Tammy	Abt. 1977	3rd great granddaughter
Freda, Gloria Ann	06 Mar 1921	Wife of great grandson
Hogan, Robert	28 Oct 1947	Husband of 2nd great granddaughter
Hunter, Colleen	14 May 1961	Wife of 2nd great grandson
McCauley, James	1849	Son

     Appendix K

Kinship Report for Stephen McCauley

Name:	Birth Date:	Relationship:
McCauley, Letitia	06 Dec 1880	Granddaughter
McCauley, Letitia Wallace	26 Jul 1885	Granddaughter
McCauley, Margaret	10 Dec 1856	Daughter
McCauley, Margaret	10 Oct 1883	Granddaughter
McCauley, Mary Ann	07 Jul 1892	Granddaughter
McCauley, Stephen	May 1817	Self
McCauley, Thomas	14 Feb 1854	Son
McCauley, Thomas Wallace	Oct 1888	Grandson
McCauley, Willis Skillman Sr.	08 Sep 1896	Grandson
McCauley, Willis Skillman Jr.	13 Jan 1922	Great grandson
McEvoy, Barbara		Wife of 2nd great grandson
Muller, August C.	22 Sep 1888	Husband of granddaughter
Muller, Marion Elaine	20 Aug 1927	Great granddaughter
Muller, Virginia Lorraine	16 Nov 1919	Great granddaughter
Plant, Kevin Figart	01 Jan 1974	3rd great grandson
Ratti, Gino John	21 Nov 1940	Husband of 2nd great granddaughter
Ratti, Mark Harry	1977	3rd great grandson
Ratti, Michael John	1975	3rd great grandson
Rosenbaum, Allison Leigh	15 Jan 1985	3rd great granddaughter
Rosenbaum, Irving	31 Mar 1949	Husband of 2nd great granddaughter
Rosenbaum, Marissa Ann	10 Jul 1987	3rd great granddaughter
Schwartz, Mae	18 Feb 1894	Wife of grandson
Skinner, Catherine Smith	20 Jul 1989	3rd great granddaughter
Skinner, Robert	07 Oct 1951	Husband of 2nd great granddaughter
Skinner, Sarah Chambers	27 Dec 1991	3rd great granddaughter
Smith, John Thomas	03 Mar 1872	Husband of granddaughter
Torpey, Martin Joseph	07 Jan 1941	Husband of 2nd great granddaughter
Wallace, Margaret	Abt. 1823	Wife
Wallace, Mary Ann	25 Nov 1854	Daughter-in-law
Wilson, Douglas Edgar	20 Jul 1964	2nd great grandson
Wilson, Edgar D.	10 Aug 1932	Husband of great granddaughter
Wilson, Margaret Elizabeth	24 Nov 1961	2nd great granddaughter
Wright, Agnes Wallace	14 Nov 1893	Granddaughter
Wright, Margaret Ann	31 Dec 1891	Granddaughter
Wright, Robert	24 Oct 1864	Son-in-law
Wright, Robert Jr.	13 Jan 1888	Grandson
Wright, Thomas Wallace	10 Apr 1890	Grandson